Our Queen Esther

Our Queen Esther

Compiled and Edited by

Lynette Bachman
Susan Coker
Sherri Stewart

Belleville, Ontario, Canada

Our Queen Esther

Copyright © 2001, Lynette Bachman,
Susan Coker, Sherri Stewart

ISBN: 1-55306-319-8

**For more information or
to order additional copies, please contact:**

Sherri Stewart
1015 San Marcos Cove
Lawrenceville, GA 30043 USA
(678) 376-1184

Essence Publishing is a Christian Book Publisher dedicated to further-
ing the work of Christ through the written word. *Epic Books* is an
imprint of *Essence Publishing*. For more information, contact:
44 Moira Street West, Belleville, Ontario, Canada K8P 1S3.
Phone: 1-800-238-6376. Fax: (613) 962-3055.
E-mail: info@essencegroup.com
Internet: www.essencegroup.com

Printed in Canada
by

Foreword

Lynette Bachman, Susan Coker, Sherri Stewart

Since the time of Job, people have been grappling with the issue, "Why do the righteous suffer?" If there were an easy answer to that question, perhaps those who suffer could bear the pain more easily. However, more often than not, no one knows why some must live with debilitating and painful diseases with no apparent cause.

Such a person is the focus of this book. Esther Smith has spent most of her adult life imprisoned in a body that prevents her from functioning to any degree. She has to depend on others for her every need. Although her mind is sharp, not a day has gone by during the past thirty years when she was not at the mercy of others. Certainly she has asked God, "Why?"

This is a book compiled by her friends who have helped her, laughed and cried with her, and watched her persevere with God's help through a seemingly endless, dark valley. Perhaps part of the answer to the question, "Why do the righteous suffer?" is found in the pages of this book. As Esther's friends and family participate in her suffering, we see how God sustains and loves His children through their circumstances. Second Corinthians 1:3,4 reads:

Praise be to the God and Father of our Lord Jesus Christ, the Father of compassion and the God of all

*comfort, who comforts us in all our troubles, so
that we can comfort those in any trouble with the
comfort we ourselves have received from God.*

This book is dedicated to Esther and her husband Joel,
and it is our hope that those who read it will be comforted
by the fact that while God may not remove the cause of our
suffering, He will provide a way to endure it with joy.

We want to thank all of Esther's friends and relatives
who have contributed to this labor of love. Esther and Joel
have always wanted to tell her story, and we have been
blessed by being part of the process. As the reader will see,
the common threads throughout the book are Esther's
steadfast joy in the midst of her circumstances and the fact
that all who have helped her have come away uplifted.

Our special thanks go out to Joshua Stewart for his help
with formatting, proofreading, scanning, downloading, and
other tasks that none of us computer illiterate types would
have been able to accomplish without his help.

In Christ,

Lynette Bachman
Susan Coker
Sherri Stewart

Beginnings

From Texas to Georgia

Saundra Brewer

The first time I actually saw Esther was when she and her husband Joel attended the same Sunday school class that I visited in 1975. It was Charlie Bradford's class. He taught the 35-50 year-old couples in the sanctuary of the Missionary Alliance Church of Lilburn, Georgia. I probably would have never noticed Esther had she and Joel not arrived late that morning. Mr. Bradford looked up from the teacher's podium with his "come on down" gesture, bidding the latecomers welcome.

"Good morning," Charlie said. "You're the Smiths, I believe. There's plenty of room. I'm just getting warmed up, so you haven't missed much."

I remember Esther's dark eyes glancing nervously over the twelve or fifteen couples staring at her. Holding tightly to Joel's arm, she forced a smile and tried to hurry her steps to an empty pew. Her gait seemed unsteady. It reminded me of a duck trying to make its way down a steep embankment. I guess I knew then that something was wrong with Esther.

Esther and I did not actually converse during that first month or so that I visited Mr. Bradford's class, but we did often exchange warm nods of greeting. It wasn't until one Monday when I saw Joel in the grocery store that I recall speaking to him for the first time. After exchanging greetings,

I casually mentioned that I looked forward to seeing him and Esther in Sunday school. Joel explained that he, Esther, and their young daughter Deana,were taking a trip to Texas to visit Esther's mother and family and would not be attending church on Sunday. I left the grocery store with no thought of God's tender plan already in the making, a divine plan that would invite me into the lives of Esther and her family.

❧

The family Esther had left in Texas before coming to Georgia in 1967 was no ordinary family. They were of Mexican and German descent. Her mother Herlinda Herrara Estrada Uribe was born May 31, 1908, in Mazatlan, Sinaloa, Mexico. She married forty-six year old Filipe Estrada when she was only thirteen. From their marriage, nine children were born. One son died during infancy. Filipe Estrada already had one daughter the same age as his young bride, as well as one son older than Herlinda. Filipe eventually brought the family to Texas so he could find work to support them. When Herlinda was pregnant with their ninth child, Filipe succumbed to a heart attack.

After Filipe's death, Herlinda was barely able to feed and clothe her family by working in a laundry, until she married Esther's father, Aniceto Uribe, in 1940. Born in 1885 in Mexico to Spanish and German parents, Aniceto lived during the time of Mexico's Diaz dictatorship and the 1910 Revolution.

Esther's father often spoke of his experiences as a teenager fighting alongside other Mexican soldiers against Pancho Villa. He told his children with pride that in 1915, the United States recognized Carranza as Mexico's president, and then a year later, the USA sent General John Pershing into Mexico to put a stop to Villa's banditry.

Aniceto brought nine of his own children into the marriage with Esther's mother. Together they had three more daughters, Esther, Hope, and Geraldine. Esther's real, half, and step-siblings eventually expanded to a count of twenty-three.

Esther recalled the memories of her father as being a mixture of strengths and weaknesses. "He was a handsome, strong man with a stature of five feet eleven inches," she said. "He was a bricklayer superintendent, and he would bring home his blueprints to read on Fridays and Saturdays. I would often look over his shoulder when he did this. The blueprints were written in Spanish and English, and he could read both languages. I learned a lot of English from this."

"He would sometimes come home drunk, and then his manner was rough," Esther remembered, "but he would take time to tell us how he had grown up in a middle-class family in Mexico, where doing the tango was his passion. Things were not always peaceful because of the tension we all felt from being in a blended family and the constant need of food, blankets, and clothes. Mom cried a lot then, and when two of her sons went off to fight in World War II, she was constantly praying for them. My dad did read the Bible, but he did not play an active role in the church until his later life after I was grown. Mom told me that Dad would sing hymns to me when I was a baby so I would go to sleep."

Esther walked when she was nine months, and she talked very well for a one-year-old. Her mother told her that she was never a sickly child. It was Esther's mom who sent her to a Baptist church when she was a small child. Esther, however, sneaked off to a Methodist church when she was in the first grade, and eventually she made a profession of faith at age twelve in that same Methodist church. For the most part, Esther attended The First Mexican Baptist Church of Lamprimeria. Here the Bible was taught in Spanish until the late 1950s when it was changed to English.

Esther credits her beginning English language skills to the Texas children she played with at an early age, and to the newspaper comics she read with her mom. Before the age of six, Esther understood a limited amount of English.

"Growing up on Howard Street in Corpus Christi was a fun time of mixed cultures," Esther recalled. "One freckled, red-haired playmate named Sally became my best friend for two years. We both attended George Evans Elementary School, and I often sneaked over to her house after school."

"Then there was a black family who lived two houses down from us," Esther continued. "Their name was Flowers, and I remember Mr. Flowers was a funeral director. I played with Joann and Carolyn Flowers until junior high. Mrs. Flowers didn't teach school until her kids were grown, but it was her influence that helped me realize that I wanted to become a teacher one day. Our families traded food a lot, and the children in the Flowers family played a big role in helping me to learn the English language. The Flowers family also introduced me to biscuits, bacon, and syrup."

"My half brother, Tito, married Ramona, whom we affectionately called Rae. I was nine when she came to our house for the first time. She had blue eyes and blond hair. Even though I associated with Anglos at school and elsewhere, this was the first time I recall that one was ever in our home. She was so nice and kind to me, and it was Rae who was instrumental in getting me to speak English correctly."

Perhaps God designed Esther's early struggles with having to learn a new culture and a new language as a way to help toughen her up for the adult life she would have to live.

Esther married Joel Smith on October 8, 1966, after they had known each other for only a month. Joel left just a month later for Vietnam and was gone for nine months.

In his absence, Esther worked in California with a construction contractor that sent equipment to Vietnam. She terminated her job as the war was ending and Joel's tour was completed. From California, the newlyweds decided to return to Joel's home state of Georgia to begin their lives together. In 1967, they drove to Texas to see Esther's family and then flew on to Georgia in September.

Esther still remembers stepping off the plane and thinking how beautiful Georgia was. "People in Georgia were extremely friendly," she said. "I wasn't used to the warm greetings that I received from Joel's family."

Her culture had been different. Kisses were reserved for very close relatives, not those she had just met. "I felt very awkward," Esther reflected. "I was conscious that no other Latinos were present. Suddenly I felt strangely alone, and to compound my agony, my new relatives took Joel and me to a nice restaurant in Atlanta for a noon meal. I wasn't hungry because I was nauseated from eating sausage on the airplane and remained nauseated for the next three months." Esther would learn that sausage was one of many foods to which she was allergic.

After leaving the grocery store in Lilburn the day I saw Joel, I focused mostly on attending to my own family's needs for the rest of the week. My husband was an absentee husband and father in that his job required him to travel out of state for a week or more at a time. I was learning that I could not do all the things I wanted to do for others because of my own responsibilities for four very active children.

It was a time when I depended upon prayer as the connective link to those who were either spiritually or physically needy. I would often go into my prayer closet just to listen to God's urgings for whom to pray for each day. It was an exciting adventure that made me more dependent upon God than myself to accomplish what seemed impossible. It was through prayer that God's plan for me to become friends with the Smith family unfolded.

When my quiet time came around on Thursday of the same week that I had seen Joel, I remember to this day, twenty-six years later, the strong pull from God to pray for the Smith family. I got down on my knees in my bedroom and just spoke a few words of general petition for Esther and her family. It probably sounded something like, "Lord, whatever the reason You have urged me to pray for the Smith family, please help them."

After my prayer for the Smiths, I really did not think much about them again until sitting in church Sunday and hearing Pastor Steinmann address the congregation with an urgent prayer request. He said that the church received a phone call on Thursday of that week from the Joel Smith family, who was visiting family in Texas. Joel revealed that his young daughter, Deana, was gravely ill with a high temperature and a kidney infection and would appreciate our prayers for her healing. The hair on my arms stood at attention. There was no question that God had given me a direct line to His mighty powers on behalf of the Smith family. I reasoned that if this family was that important to God, then they would also become a priority for me.

With an open invitation from God to visit the Smiths when they returned from Texas, Esther and I soon became good friends. I discovered early on in our friendship that she was dealing with more pain than most of us experience in a lifetime. Her body had suddenly become her worst enemy. Pain took over her whole body and bombarded her constantly. It would not allow her to turn, sit, stand, or bend. Doctors diagnosed her condition as rheumatoid psoriatic arthritis.

At first, doctors gave Esther hope in their promises that hip replacements and knee operations would diminish her suffering. I remember how glad Esther was that something could be done for her pain. Even though Dr. Howard Krone explained that there was a chance that after the operations, she might never walk again, he did assure her that she would have less pain. Nothing was further from the truth. Esther not only suffered excruciating agony after each operation, but all the medications caused her body to go into more rebellion. "I could feel every wrinkle in the sheet on which I was lying," she said.

Esther's prognosis was more despairing. Rheumatologists finally told her that nothing could be done to improve her condition. Up until that time, every doctor she had seen had, at least, given her hope if she would just follow their instructions and specifications. She had believed and trusted them. After her operations and all the allergic reactions to medications, the surgeons told her that her bones had calcified and nothing else could be done, but the pain was still there, only more intensified.

God had given Esther a special verse to cling to before her hospital stay.

Yet those who wait for the Lord will gain new strength; they will mount up with wings like eagles; they will run and not get tired, they will walk and not become weary (Isaiah 40: 31).

Following the surgery, that verse was pushed aside, as she had to come to terms with her arthritis consuming her whole life, and the fact that she could do nothing to stop it. God gave her another verse.

And if I go and prepare a place for you, I will come again and receive you to Myself; that where I am, there you may be also (John 14:3).

This was a verse that Esther associated with funerals.

The day Esther rationalized that death would be a way of ridding herself of all pain was the day she attempted suicide. Yet God had other plans for Esther, so He preserved her life. With God's help, she gained a more personal meaning of John 14:3. A revived Esther felt reassured by the love of Jesus because *"...that where I am, there you may be also,"* meant that God would remain with her, no matter how much pain or disability she would have to endure. She knew that she could endure with Him, but not without Him. This was a spiritual victory that Esther would often share with those she met.

As time progressed, nothing physical came easy for Esther, especially when it involved the tasks that most wives and mothers perform. She often lamented about her shortcomings

How thankful Esther has always been that God gave her a persistent nature. Through the years, Esther has reluctantly given up her independence. She can no longer walk, eat, bathe, use the bathroom, or function normally without assistance. Even today when things are especially bad for her, she never surrenders to her handicap. She still boldly declares that she doesn't know how to give up.

There have been many friends and family members who have rallied behind Esther. Many of those people have created memories for me that I shall never forget. It is almost impossible for me to think of Esther without thinking of her husband Joel. A man of rare qualities, he has always been by her side. He has cried, laughed, comforted, assisted, and remained faithful to his wife. When he speaks of his family, he always praises God for the blessings He has given to them. Joel smiles whenever he talks about Esther. He is God's gift to her.

Another person I was privileged to meet was Esther's mother. Mrs. Uribe seemed such a small package to have been so full of many special gifts. Even though she could not speak English, she and I understood each other. She had a wonderful sense of humor. It was a challenge for Esther to translate her words without giving in to hysterical laughter. When I first met Mrs. Uribe, I was surprised to see how small a woman she was. I used hand gestures to indicate her tiny stature. With a twinkle in her eye, she motioned for me to be seated and then stood over me patting my head. In an instant, she had brought me below her level. When I acquiesced with a smile, she hugged me with a pair of arms that would have dwarfed Wilt Chamberlain!

Once we had become friends, I couldn't wait to ask Mrs. Uribe why she had borne so many children, especially since instant, she had brought me below her level. When I acquiesced with a smile, she hugged me with a pair of arms that would have dwarfed Wilt Chamberlain!

Once we had become friends, I couldn't wait to ask Mrs. Uribe why she had borne so many children, especially since the husbands she had married already had families. I will never forget her chuckle before she gave me a rather short answer in Spanish. It was a while before Esther controlled her laughter enough to translate, "We didn't have TV."

Of all Esther's friends, Susan Coker has been one of the more faithful. Most of us have had just a season with Esther and then moved from the center of her daily needs. This has not been true for Susan. Although she has been working full-time for the last ten or so years, she has remained on call for Esther. I know there are others in Esther's life who have been equally involved, but she is the one that keeps all of us from Esther's past up-to-date on the Smith family. Susan's love for Esther is one of the best examples of the Jonathan and David friendship that I know of.

There are so many blessings I have personally gained from sharing a small part of my life with my dear friend Esther. She taught me courage. She challenged my own faith in changing the meaning of "hopelessness" to "hopeful." She taught my youngest child the meaning of compassion for people in wheelchairs. She made me look for blessings in my own life that I had never seen before I met her. Her walk in this life has been more "grace-full" than anyone I have ever met.

Saundra Brewer now lives in Florida and continues to contribute her gift of writing to her church in the form of plays and skits.

A Glimpse of
Esther's Early Years

Hope Kelly

Esther was born a small baby with blue eyes and blond hair. Everybody teased my mom because Esther was so fair. My dad was very fair and had hazel eyes. Esther was also never sick as a young girl.

We lived in a stucco house that our daddy built on Howard Street. It had a beautiful red cement porch. People thought we were wealthy, but we were not. My daddy was a bricklayer. He came to the United States from Mexico at the age of thirteen. He never went to school, but he somehow learned to read and write both English and Spanish. It was amazing that he became one of the greatest bricklayers. Other builders were engineers, but my daddy learned by doing the trade.

We never knew our daddy as a young man. He was twenty years older than our mother, and he was more like a grandfather to us. Daddy always gave us the same dolls every year at Christmas. I always got the black-haired doll, Geraldine got the brown-haired one, and Esther got the blond one. I guess that's the way he remembered us and kept us in his mind!

As we got older, we grew to love and respect people. Mother always taught us to respect and help older people. We helped her older friends across the street, took them to doctors, and helped them in many other ways. Mother was young; she was about thirty-five when Esther was born. Of course, she had already borne eight children by her first husband, who had died and left her a widow.

Although our mother couldn't read, she could quote Scripture by chapter and verse. She listened to preachers on the radio, and she learned Bible verses from them by memory. She would tell us what to do or how to behave and quote a book, chapter, and verse. When we looked it up, she was always right!

We girls were one year apart. Our mother was very quiet, not open about telling us anything about the "birds and the bees," and we didn't ask! We didn't know when we were children about all the troubles she had, and she never told us. She kept everything inside, and Esther is a lot like her. Mommy was always positive and upbeat about life and never showed hurt feelings or anxiety. Like any blended family today, we had our ups and downs, but we stayed together! When we found out later about the problems, we said to each other, "It's not our fault—we were just babies!"

Esther always enjoyed going barefoot in the winter and the summer when we were children. Mom got after her saying, "Don't be lazy. You could get a disease that might cause you not to be able to walk!"

Esther would say, "Oh, Mom! I don't like socks, and it feels good to go barefoot in the sand!"

Esther also loved the water. When we were little, our daddy would sometimes take us to the ocean bay. We could not swim, so we were never allowed to go into the deep water. Daddy always said, "Swim only by the sand!"

When we got old enough to drive, we used to go to Padre Island with a carload of girls, sometimes eight or ten friends piled in the car! It wasn't against the law, and the police just smiled and waved to us.

We three girls were always very close. In the summers we played together all the time. Esther was always the teacher, businesswoman, or secretary. She always had paper and a pencil. Geraldine had a grocery store. She was always selling something like Kool-Aid. I was always working with children. Since we've grown up, Geraldine has always been in sales, either insurance, furniture, or Avon. I am a paraprofessional in the schools, working with four-year-old children. Not surprisingly, Esther grew up to be an office worker.

When she was thirteen years old, she started to work in the Waco Food Store as a cashier. She was the type of person everyone fell in love with because she was so outgoing, joyful, and positive. Esther's supervisor, Mrs. Hannaway, liked Esther so much she used to get Esther to rub her feet! When our sister, Geraldine, and I were working there, we would be mopping the floor and doing other hard work, and we would look, and see Esther rubbing Mrs. Hannaway's feet or neck. We would ask, "How did you get selected to do that, while we are working so hard?"

Esther would say, "I'm working too!"

When she was fifteen years old, our daddy bought us a 1954 red and white Chevy. People thought we were wealthy because a lot of people didn't have cars in those days. But I think because my daddy was old, he was looking to the future when he wouldn't be able to drive us around, and he knew we would have to drive ourselves to work. He sent me to drivers' school to learn how to drive. But Esther and Geraldine didn't go. They were more daring than I was. They used to sneak the car out and drive around the block teaching themselves to drive. I told them, "You shouldn't be doing this because you don't have a driver's license!"

Esther would say, "Shh, we're learning to drive!"

The police never put us in jail. We never got caught. I think the police were kinder in those days!

After the job at the food store, Esther got a better one at Handy Cleaners on Saturdays and in the summers. She was in customer service and was a cashier. Then she got a job working in a daycare as a teacher. In those days, you didn't have to have a certificate to teach.

Esther enjoyed the hobby of reading. She would read anything she could find...newspapers, magazines, anything. She loved music, too, and she loved to dance. Her favorite thing to do was to dance the "mashed potato," and she was very good at it!

Esther was always a very positive young girl, very joyful. She believed you could do anything if you put your mind to it. She was very smart and a straight-A student. Her favorite subjects were Math and English. She never had to study, whereas Geraldine and I always did have to study to make our grades. She was a great listener. She teased us and said, "Why study? I listen in class and don't have to study." We did too, but we still had to study! One time we took Physical Education together. I studied and she didn't. She made 100 percent on the test, and I only made 95 percent.

While I was dating my husband-to-be, Bill Kelly, from age seventeen until I married him at nineteen, I was never allowed to go out with him alone. Esther and Geraldine went with us everywhere we went. I was always like the mom, wearing my watch and saying at ten o'clock, "It's time to go home."

But Esther would say, "No, we just got here!" and Bill would agree with her! Bill was always a gentleman. Even before I liked him as a boyfriend, I went out with him as a friend, and my sisters always went, too. I could trust him to take care of the three of us.

When Esther graduated from high school, she received a grant to go to college for four years. For some reason, Daddy didn't want her to go away, so he hid the grant in a locked cedar chest. Esther never knew about this grant until our father died much later, and we were going through his papers.

Esther went to live with her brother, Tito, and sister-in-law, Mona, in Wichita Falls after high school. She hoped that Tito would be able to help her go to college. She worked and went to college for about two years, but never got her degree. This was something she always wanted, but it was so hard working and going to school. And to think that she could have had this scholarship for four years! But she became very skillful at office work. In school we never took band or any other subject that was just for our entertainment. Our daddy said we should take classes that would help us get a job when we finished school. So Esther took typing, shorthand, and bookkeeping. Esther was good at being a secretary, but her strong desire to get a college degree was never realized.

Esther has always been a perfectionist! When she came to visit my house, I would tell her, "Esther, my house is clean on the outside, but don't look in the closets!"

When I had some surgery, and I had to sit around the house not doing anything, I would see the dirt on the baseboards and tell my husband to clean it. He said, "Why are you noticing this now, and you never did before?" I think that Esther must become very frustrated when she sees the dust accumulating and can't do a thing about it.

Esther is a very sensitive girl, although she doesn't let anyone see this. Like our mother, Esther has never shown her emotions. She expresses herself very well, never ugly. But she does let you know what she is feeling! Her body may not be able to move, but her mind is always working. As Deana was growing up, she taught her how to clean house and how to cook. She also taught Joel how to cook! This is how she taught Deana to cook when she was very young. "Deana, do this, and then do this." Esther still runs her household from her chair. She knows that Joel and Deana have always depended on her to do this. However, they are both very good cooks and housekeepers now. They can manage now unsupervised, but that does not mean that she has stopped overseeing the jobs!

As an adult, Esther has shown me that no matter what kind of trouble we have, we must put it in the hands of God. I ask her, "How do you go on day by day? I couldn't cope with sickness all the time like you do."

Esther replies, "I put God first, He gives me the strength to keep going for Joel and Deana." I have never heard her complain. When I call to ask how she's doing, she always says, "I'm doing great. I get better and better all the time." Only one time this year she cried on the phone saying, "I'm so tired!" I told her that she couldn't get tired, because she still has a lot of things to do. When my brothers and sisters say they are tired, they are talking about going to Heaven to be with Mom, and I don't want Esther to talk like this.

Esther has a special spot for all her brothers and sisters. We have always been close to our mom and dad's other children, and the reason is because we have Christ in common. We know how to work things out. When we get together, we sing hymns, read the Bible, pray, and quote Scriptures. Before Mom died, she told all of us to look after each other, and we do. We call back and forth and pray over the phone when we are hurting. Esther is the one I call a lot. She's my life, like my second mom. If she ever leaves, I'll be so empty. She keeps me going. She is so special and so strong. She always says, "This will be OK."

I make her laugh and say, "Things will work out, Esther. We'll trust in God." She is so close to me. I call her almost every week.

I am very thankful for Esther's friends who have been so helpful to her for all these years. They are very special people, so I refer to them as "people from the Bible." By that I mean that most people don't find friends like the ones Esther has. I have lived in a lot of different places, and I have never seen friends like hers—people she can tell her problems to, depend on, and trust. I am also thankful for all the people from her church. There is no way that I can ever repay Esther's friends and church family for all they have done for her, except by praying for them, and that is what I do.

Esther has always been very positive, She never gives up. Her motto is, "Where there's a will, there's a way." Esther is an inspiration because she lives out the truth that no matter how bad things are, there's still hope. She says, "All these years I'm praying, and if I'm not walking, there's a reason for it. But I know I'll be walking on streets of Glory someday with Mom."

Hope Kelly, Esther's next-to-youngest sister, is a para-professional in the school system in Arlington, Texas. She feels she was placed there by God to minister to the children.

A Sister's Faith

Geraldine Perez

My sister, Hope, has told much of the story of our growing up years with Esther. I want to agree with her that Esther has always been very joyful, has always laughed, is very smart, and was never sick.

We grew up in a Christian home. Even when our parents couldn't go to church because of my father's work schedule, our mother always saw to it that we went to the Baptist church that was near our house. Of course, Baptists in those days believed that dancing and going to parties was a sin, so Esther often sneaked off to the Methodist church that was right across the street. Hope and I always followed her. The pastor, Brother Dickson, was very nice to the youth, and they were always having parties and giving us candy! We liked to go to their Halloween parties where we bobbed for apples. Our father would catch us and say, "No, don't go to the Methodist church because we are Baptists!" But we went anyway. I hated being a Baptist! I would have preferred to be a Catholic so I could dance!

Once we were going to a dance at a military base where Hope's fiancé, Bill Kelly, was going to get us in. He didn't have a car at the time, so we drove our car. I think I was driving. I was going too fast, and the car flipped over. There were no seat belts in those days, but by the grace of God, we were not hurt. The police came and took all the information and let us go. They were very kind to us. We thought the incident was over, but unfortunately for us, our father saw the report of the accident the next day on the television news report. When we realized this, we said, "Oh, no, we're in trouble," and we were! He got after us and took the car away for a while. Father wouldn't let Bill come around the house for some time after that.

Our father was very old-fashioned and strict. He was quite old when we were growing up—in his seventies. He didn't let Bill come in to see Hope every time he felt like it. Sometimes he was only allowed to come onto the porch and talk to our father. His attitude was this: "You marry my daughter, and then you can see her whenever you want!" His English was limited, but he always managed to get his point across!

Another time we had gone to a party or dance and were supposed to be home at a certain time. I don't remember which of us was driving, but we ran into a ditch and could not get the car out! We didn't want our father to know what had happened, and somebody, maybe Bill, helped us out. Our niece was with us, so we had to tell her parents why we were late. Our mother didn't tell our father because he was asleep, but he eventually found out, and we got into a lot of trouble. We weren't supposed to be going to a dance because we were Baptists.

When we got older, Hope married Bill, and Esther moved off to live with our half brother, Tito, in Wichita Falls. I married a Catholic man when I was about twenty-one, but I lived with my parents while he was in Vietnam. We bought a house after he came home, but the marriage ended in divorce when I was thirty-two. Those were hard years for me. I learned the difference between going to church and having a personal relationship with Jesus Christ during those times. I began going to a non-denominational church, where I discovered that there is a lot more to Christianity than just being saved. After my divorce, I continued to live in my house, but I spent a great deal of time at my parents' home taking care of them. In fact, during the last two years of my mother's life, I was at their house every day and even had to give up my job in order to take care of her.

In the early years when I was raising my children, Esther would come to visit our mother, and I would see her then. Mother cried every time she came when she saw Esther in such a bad physical condition.

In 1997, I was diagnosed with lymphoma cancer in the spine. At first they thought it was arthritis, and I had to battle the demon of fear that I might have what Esther has. When they operated, the doctors told me I would never walk again because they had cut deeply to remove the tumor they had found. But I knew that God was in control, that He was my healer, and that *"by His stripes I am healed."* Esther often called to see how I was, and I would encourage her, saying everything would be all right. This was not positive thinking, as the doctors wanted to call it, but positive faith in God. I claimed Mark 11:23, which says,

> *Therefore I tell you, whatever you ask for in prayer, believe that you have received it, and it will be yours.*

If He says something in His Word, it must be so! I have had no recurrence of the cancer for four years, and I am walking again after spending eight months in bed. I give God all the praise and glory for my healing and my salvation!

Seeing my faith for my circumstances gave Esther courage to face her own. I told Esther, "We have to be in God's presence, not just in church. I stand on the Scriptures. Don't worry about me." Esther's faith has grown, but she still calls me for her prayer needs.

I eventually married a wonderful man, Abelardo Perez. He was so good to me when I had cancer. He took me for chemotherapy and took care of me. I was afraid to marry after my first bad experience, but we married in 1998, and have been married now for three years.

The thing that keeps Esther going is her faith in God. Esther was always very independent and very smart. To be confined like she is, she would never make it without her faith. It is very hard to live the kind of life she lives. We were blessed to be brought up believing in God. Our mother was not educated, but she was very wise and had a strong faith in God, which she imparted to all of us. She didn't leave us money, but she gave us a heritage of love and faith that we will never forget. I always tell people that I am the woman I am today because of God and my mother. Esther will tell you the same thing. We have learned that we cannot question God or His motives in our suffering, but that He is in control of everything, and He knows what He is doing.

I would like to thank all of Esther's friends in Georgia who have helped her. We would have been there for her if we didn't live so far away. It's comforting to know that she is not alone.

Geraldine Perez is Esther's youngest sister and lives in Corpus Christi, Texas. A cancer survivor, she literally is a walking miracle and devoted Christian who, as she says, is a "Baptist with a Pentecostal experience!"

More Family History

Becky Edwards

I am Esther's oldest stepsister. We had the same mother but different fathers. My father was Mexican, whereas Esther's was half-Mexican and half-Spanish. Our mother's parents knew the infamous Mexican bandit PanchoVilla. When they heard that he was riding into town, they would hide all the children in a cave in the mountains.

They especially had to protect the young girls, including our mother, from Villa's men. Our grandparents actually fed this man and his entourage and were good to them because when he came, he would bring cattle, and they didn't have any beef. They said he was not as bad a character as people thought but was more like a Robin Hood of that day!

My dad died when I was eleven, and we were never able to be children after that. We never played. We had to work outside the home to bring in money. I went to live with a Jewish couple as a nanny for their children. I learned more from them than anyone! They teased me by saying, "We would make you a Jew, but you'd never look it because of your nose!" They told me to hold my head up and be proud that I was Mexican. "They may not like you here," they said, "but they don't like *us* in New York!"

I didn't even know I was born in Mexico until I was fifteen years old. Mother brought us to the United States in

1926, when I was about two months old, and you only had to pay a nickel to cross the border. She was very young and uneducated. She had married my father when she was just thirteen.

I got married when I was seventeen years old. When I left home, Esther was just a baby. We moved to Maryland for four years, but then we came back to Corpus Christi. By that time, Esther was in school. I had my own children and a very busy life. We were a very large family, but we visited often. My younger sister, Orfa, used to play with Esther, as did my brother, Raul, and sister, Minerva. My children are a few years younger than Esther, so they never really played together.

I have always admired Esther because of her Christianity and the fact that she was such a hard worker who excelled in school. If Esther could move around, she would be doing a lot of things. She has always had such a good vocabulary. She was in church all the time as a young girl. I admire her because she is like Queen Esther in the Bible. I tell her, "You have so much pain, and yet you keep on going." She is a faithful wife and a good mother. She has married a wonderful Christian man who takes good care of her. I have learned from my own experiences that suffering makes you stronger. Esther's suffering has made her strong.

Esther's oldest stepsister, Becky Edwards, lives in Esther's hometown, Corpus Christi. A member of a Baptist church there, she has always been active in helping with the senior citizens, and her home is always open to visiting missionaries.

My Wife, Mary Esther

Joel Smith

I met Mary Esther Uribe on September 7, 1966. She was a pleasant lady. I was pleased to have met such a sweet little woman as she was, and over the years, she has managed to stay the same. My friend, Mike Estok, told me about a bunch of girls who lived in the apartment close by the Navy base where I was stationed in California. One night he took me over there. Esther and a few other girls let us in. When I first saw her, I was impressed. I knew she was special. We all decided to play cards and eat popcorn. I wanted to come back and see her, so I asked for a date. The next day, I walked over to Mary Esther's apartment. We stayed there, drank coffee, and just talked. She told me that she was forty-two years old when she was really only twenty-four. She was trying to tell me that we just needed to be friends. Then I asked her to go dancing and out to eat with me. During this time, I knew I was going to have to go to Vietnam. I was twenty-three. I had already volunteered to go into the Seabees. I knew that I wanted a relationship with Mary Esther. I wanted it to be permanent. I asked her, "If I give you a ring, would you be faithful to me till I get back?"

She said, "I don't know. I don't know how faithful you will be to me."

So I said, "How about if we get married later?" But I meant right then! She said yes, so we planned a date for the wedding. We planned it for a Saturday so the family could come. Esther had to plan a wedding in just a few weeks. We got married in a Navy chapel in Port Hueneme, on October 8, 1966.

We didn't have a honeymoon because we didn't have much money, and I was in the service. We later found out that the military would have given us a week's leave if we had known to ask for it. We spent our first night together in our apartment. The next morning our friends wanted us to go bowling with them. We didn't want to go with them. Bowling was not on our mind at that moment.

Our dating time took place after our wedding. One of the first places we went was to El Monte in southern California to meet Esther's relatives. I liked all the relatives. They wanted to fix a nice meal for us. We had a good time together.

When we got back from southern California, it was time for me to finish my training and prepare to go to Vietnam. When I was in Vietnam, they set up a ham radio station so I could talk to Esther. It was nice to hear her voice. I was over there for nine months. When my R&R came due, we were able to go to Hawaii. Esther flew there to meet me. They gave us the bridal suite in a nice hotel. We were on the seventh floor overlooking Diamond Head, a large rock that jutted out into the water. It was always visible whether it was cloudy or not.

While Esther was waiting for me to arrive, she would go down to the beach. A man wanted to teach her the hula. She liked learning and doing the hula dance. While we were in Hawaii, we were finally able to enjoy our honeymoon. It was a most pleasant time. The weather went from monsoon to almost perfect weather. In the evenings, we went out to dance. Esther knew I didn't know how to fast dance, and she told me she wanted to fast dance and not to stop her. She loved to dance.

When the honeymoon was over, I had to go back to Vietnam, and Esther returned to our apartment. While I was gone, Esther worked on the base as the head of a typing pool. She could type seventy words per minute. When she wanted to have some fun, she went out with our old crowd. One of the things she did was go grunion hunting at the beach. One time the guys threw her into the cold water while the grunions were running. She didn't like catching them because they were really slimy.

I remember several times seeing Esther wearing a tight dress and high heels while riding on a bike. She used to ride her bike to work. She didn't like to walk. She told me the story about another time when she wore a tight dress. She went to get gas in the car. That was back when they had full service stations. The gas attendant was washing the windows, and finally he looked in the window and said to Esther, "You have nice legs." Right then she thought to herself, *I can't wear this dress again*! So I asked my mom to make Esther some new clothes that would be more modest.

Esther and I had a baby daughter born February 17, 1971. We named her Deana Marie. Dean is my middle name so we added an "a" on and called her Deana. Esther's first name is Mary so we changed the "y" to "ie" for Marie. She was such a sweet child who loved to sing and dance like her mother. She has been a lot of help to both her mother and me for the past twenty-six years.

Mary Esther has been my companion, willing to help me when I went back to school. For a short while, Esther worked at the IRS, and Deana went to day care. Later when she worked at Macy's at night, I would take care of Deana. Esther worked in the Department of Agriculture in 1968, as an interpreter translator from Spanish to English for her boss. She was happy and energetic about her work because she saw good results being done. Esther worked there for about two and a half years.

Mary Esther has been my friend as long as we have known each other. It has been a privilege I will always cherish to have met her. I have learned to appreciate that care and love is what you need. The fact is that you need to know how to care and love your mate each day, regardless of their health. You will find that it is possible with the Lord's help to have a genuine love for each other. Esther is the reason that I have been able to carry on. You will understand once you meet her. She will show you how important it is to carry on each day. Esther is the lady who has God's peace and the knowledge of His love and care, and wants to share this with everyone she meets. Knowing Esther has been, and will be, just one reason for me to keep on trying to live.

She is always trying to make our lives better because she understands the importance of carrying on an active life. Esther has been in that wheelchair for at least twenty-four years because of failing joints. She still continues to enjoy each new day. Esther knows that every day has a part to play in our lives, and knowing this helps us to enjoy every day to the fullest. She can tell you that Jesus has made our relationship much stronger because He has allowed us to commit our time to each other. Because of His love, we are committed to one another, and the Lord honors that commitment.

Joel has been a faithful, loving, and caring husband and father for thirty-five years.

35

Remembering Growing Up

Deana Smith and Renae Little Reese

OUR YOUNGER YEARS

As long as Deama and Renae can remember, they have known each other and been best friends. They met in Renae's front yard when Renae was seven and Deana was eight. It was "friends at first sight." After that they were inseparable. Phone calls were heard on either side. "Can Deana come out and play?" and vice versa. Esther (Mom) was a big part in their growing relationship as girls.

DEANA: I remember times when Renae would come over, and Mom would say, "Is that Renae?" When I said yes, Mom would say, "Well, have Renae come back to see me." We would both go back to Mom's bedroom, where she would usually be resting, and her face would light up because her "second daughter" had come over to play with her first! There were times when Mom would interrupt our playtime by asking us to help her go to the bathroom, and we would both help her and not think anything of it.

RENAE: Some of my fondest childhood memories were at Deana's house. We used our creative imaginations to be everything from detectives to painters. I remember one time Deana's mom got us to pretend to be maids, so that we would clean her room... and we did. It took us *all* day, but we had fun "pretending." Esther was always curious as to what we were playing that day. We went through a phase where we were famous dancers, and we would practice our dance routines for weeks. Then we would help Esther to the living room, and we would perform at least three times with her as our audience. One time she even let us use her good china for a dance/skit. She always wanted to help us in our playtime.

OUR TEENAGE YEARS

DEANA: I remember coming home after school in high school and going straight back to my mom's room and telling her about my day, including all the details of what had happened. Her face would light up when I entered the room and continued to do so as I talked. Even when I had bad things to discuss with her, her face would be full of encouragement.

Those years had lots of bad times sprinkled with good. They were often spent by visiting her in the hospital or calling her there. She was always full of encouragement for me. She let me know that no matter how much pain she was going through, she was always there to listen to whatever I had to say. I can remember one specific year, the beginning of my tenth grade, when I stayed with Renae and her family because my parents did not want me to spend a lot of time alone. I stayed with them for about five or six weeks and became their "third daughter."

When I graduated from high school, there was a party at my house. My parents were so excited that I could finally move on to college. My mom was so proud of me! She had always wanted the very best for me, and that was only the beginning.

RENAE: As Deana and I grew up, we did not spend as many hours in the house. Most of our time was spent after school walking up and down the street with a boom box and just talking. During my high school years, Deana moved off to college, and I took on the role of "bathroom monitor." I always wanted to help Esther, but sometimes her calls came at the end of very important TV shows. I knew I had to go then, or else, and sometimes I didn't always have the best attitude walking down to the house. But I always left an hour later in a good mood. Esther would always ask me how everything in my life was going, including current crushes, and she remembered it all. She always gave me wise advice and encouragement in all the areas I was concerned about. She acted (and asked questions) like a mother and always made me feel good about myself. She appreciated me, and I appreciated her.

THE COLLEGE YEARS, OUR BERT AND ERNIE ADVENTURES

Renae joined Deana as her roommate at Toccoa Falls College. When they were trying to decide what special attributes their room would have and how to decorate, Bert and Ernie kept reoccurring in their minds. Bert and Ernie were roommates and were the best of friends, and they felt the same. Deana was Bert, and Renae was Ernie. They decorated their entrance and bathroom to the hilt with those characters to remind them of their friendship.

DEANA: As I mentioned earlier, my going to college was just the beginning of all the good things that my mom saw for my life. She took great interest in making sure that financial aid was taken care of for my schooling. She was always very encouraging. She wanted to know what was happening, and what I was doing in class and out of class.

The stories I told her about my friends and what we did fascinated her. She met several of my other friends in college and was always open to having everyone come over to the house on special occasions.

I remember one specific Christmas when I came home. On Christmas Day, because of Mom's connections with church groups, I was given all the products that I needed for the next school year. When I graduated, she wanted to sing the "Hallelujah Chorus" because she had fought for me to graduate when I did!

RENAE: Esther continued to encourage me throughout my college years as well. I would chat with her for a moment when Deana called home from the dorm room. We would visit and see each other on holidays and, of course, summers. We had more adult conversations then, like whom did I love, and what was I going to do with the rest of my life? As Deana has mentioned, although I was not her real daughter, she took me on as hers, and I could always tell when she was proud of me and when she would rather that I had done something a different way. She continued to give me wise advice.

NOW WE'RE "GROWN-UPS"

Neither girl has given Esther a grandchild yet, and she is not happy about this point!

DEANA: My mom has always been accepting of where I was and whom I was with. Of course, in the beginning I chose one set of friends, and now I have a variety of friends. I moved out for the final time when I was twenty-seven years old. I was furious at my parents at the time because I felt that they were trying to keep me at home. I understand that since I am the only child, it was hard for them to let me leave the nest. But we both knew it was time for me to move on. Mom has come to understand that I need my space, and I finally am coming to her as a grown-up, calling her every week to find out what's going on with them and to give them an update on me.

RENAE: I hardly ever get to see or talk to Esther now. I am busy with my husband, and our careers and businesses keep us apart. Every now and then I get to talk on the phone to her, or I go by in person. I'm usually there for an hour or more, and now our relationship has changed a little bit. She still listens to everything that is going on with me. Even though I have become more mature, I listen to her just as much. But I also get to give wise advice, which I learned from one of the best teachers—Esther herself.

IN CONCLUSION:

RENAE: As my second mom, you have filled in where needed with love and support as I have grown up. You have raised a wonderful daughter whom I call my best friend. Without her, my childhood wouldn't have been nearly as memorable. Thanks for having Deana, for living on my street, and loving me as a daughter. I look forward to more special talks with you!

Love, Renae

DEANA: I have grown up with one of the greatest women that I have ever known. We had our differences and our agreements. Our differences were highlighted at times more than our agreements, but I always knew that our relationship was intact. As I look back, I can honestly say that God has blessed me. I believe I have turned out to be more of a woman that my mom would be proud of, than if she had been perfectly healthy. Thank you, Mom.

One hundred kisses, Deana

Renae Little Reese has been a third-grade teacher at Perimeter Christian School for the last four years. Deana Smith now lives in Arlington, Texas, and works in corporate world.

Love from Joel's Family

Donald L. Herndon

My association with and memories of Esther go back some twenty-five to thirty years. Esther is my niece-in-law, married to my nephew, Joel Smith. Esther has been an invalid for most of the years since her marriage to Joel. Her illnesses have not been easy for her. In fact, she has suffered long and has had much pain.

Esther, you have been a source of inspiration to many people, both your family and your church. Your joy expressed while in pain has been and is truly remarkable. Your radiance has been far beyond all expectations. Your faith has remained strong and your hope is sure.

It would seem to me appropriate to commend Joel at this time. As your life, Esther, has been lived in suffering, so Joel's life has been lived in faithfulness to you. His continuing love and patience has been and is a blessing to his family. He has demonstrated true love and commitment to his marriage.

Know that your family loves you both. I especially commend you on your Christian faith.

Donald L. Herndon of Duluth, Georgia, is Joel's uncle and a retired United Methodist Church Minister.

The Originals

From One of the Originals

Edna Bryan Reeves

I first met Esther shortly after Deana was born. We all attended a Bible study at Norma Fleming's home. We had attended Lilburn First Baptist for a short period of time, and I had seen her and her family there. That was in the early 1970s. We later moved to Arlene Smith's house in Mimosa Estates, and I don't remember Esther attending the Bible study there. But that was a long time ago, and I was not even young then!

In the mid- to late 1970s, Esther and her family started attending Lilburn Alliance Church. Someone at her church told her that we had a good outreach at LAC. Emmie Loften and Saundra Brewer told some of us that Esther desperately needed help during the day, that most of the time she didn't eat lunch because she was in such a bad condition that she could not open her cabinets. They suggested that we get some people to go daily to help her. It was Saundra, Emmie, Susan Coker, myself, and someone else (there's that senior moment again!) Some time later she was put under the umbrella of the deaconesses. At first it wasn't easy to get people to work, but later we had many volunteers because those of us who went told others that it was not hard because of Esther's wonderful attitude. She was always upbeat and a joy to be around. The only thing the job required was to fix her lunch and have fellowship with her until about an hour before Deana arrived home from school. So things really smoothed out, and we had about twenty ladies at a time going to meet these needs.

In November 1979, I lost my beloved husband of twenty-seven years, so in 1980, I gave as much time as possible to Esther. For the next nine years, I was involved with Esther until I married again in 1987, then moved to the mountains in 1988 because of my husband's retirement. Esther wanted me to be happy and had prayed for a husband for me. She said if she had it to do over, she might not have prayed that way—at least she would have prayed for me to stay in Lilburn! She, Joel, and Deana came to visit us a couple of times, and she did like it here in Blue Ridge.

We had some wonderful times together. She and I shared our innermost thoughts and problems. You could do that because you knew that it would go no further. She probably knew me better than anyone I have ever known. She was a great listener. She also shared her wants, thoughts, and problems with me. I would tell her that I hated having to do all the things we did, since I never wanted to be a nurse, and here she was trying to make one out of me! But I did do some fun things. I love to decorate, and she allowed me to do that. I thought one day about how she had to look at the same things day after day, and how I would feel if it were me. So I made curtains, dust ruffles, and drapes. I wallpapered, and some of us even painted. Once when she was in the hospital, I made curtains for her den and told her that was her flowers for being in the hospital—well, they *were* floral!

One time I talked her into hiring a girl who was living with me. This young girl had a son about two years of age.

The reason she was living with me was because of an abusive husband. But as often happens, she returned to her husband, and while out with him one day, she told him where Esther lived and that she had worked for her. Things did not work out, so Robbin was back with me and wanted to work for Esther again. I took her to Esther's and returned home. About one hour later, someone was at my front door. That someone at my door was a policeman. The husband had kidnapped the child,from Esther's house. Robbin was screaming, and of course, Esther couldn't even know what was going on, since she was still in bed in the back of the house. Esther called, and I wasn't home. She knew I had brought Robbin to her house in my robe and didn't think I would go anywhere like that, so she sent the police to check on me. I had gone next door briefly to tell my sister-in-law something. Anyway, Bob Roseveare said he didn't understand how two nice ladies like Esther and myself could be involved with such a shady thing with police involved!

She was the first person I knew who had a hip replacement. The first one didn't work, so she had to have it done again. Ever the pleasant Esther! Another time she went to North Carolina for six weeks trying to find help. She found there were certain foods that she should not eat. Two I remember were apples, which she loved, and pork. After that, she was again at Emory where they put pins in her thighs and calves and tried to straighten her legs, as she was almost in a fetal position. They would move the bar a fraction every so often. It was very painful and did not work. I think she was later told that she should have sued for this torture.

It was after that when she had the hip replaced, then later her knees, as well as her knuckles. Her knuckles had to be replaced because she could not use the arm brace crutches because her hand was completely closed from the arthritis. How many of us would have the joy of the Lord all the years that Esther suffered from this disablement? How many husbands would have loved and shown compassion for their mates after so many years of watching that loved one suffer as Joel does? I never saw anything but love and tenderness toward Esther by Joel Smith. Surely God has something special for these two.

I have said that Esther was always upbeat. Only one time did I see her down. She had been in the hospital at Snellville and stayed, I think, two weeks, so I went to see her after she got home. I walked in expecting to see a great improvement. However, there was still loose skin in her eyebrows from the psoriasis. I was shocked and said, "Oh, Esther!" She started crying, and we had a good crying session, and I believe we prayed. How discouraging to spend time in the hospital and still have your skin falling off! But our God is faithful and used that to help Esther greatly. I was sharing how bad she was with Glynis Miller. She had recently gone to work at Emory and told me that she could be helped with something that was very new at Emory. Of course I called Esther and told her. She got her doctor to enter her at Emory. Two days later I went to see her. Her skin looked like a new baby. We cried again, but for joy. Thank you, Lord! They put her in a suit like astronauts wear with the cream on her skin, which she still uses, I think. She had to wear it for twenty-four hours, and what a difference it made!

I also remember how Esther always wanted to acknowledge those who had helped her each year with a Christmas luncheon. She would never allow us to help. Her late mother-in-law, Edna Smith, would fix the meal, and we would have a wonderful time of fellowship. Each of us would get a

Christmas ornament or something usually made by Esther and Edna. I have a bell made of pearls and gold beads that Esther made. I treasure it each year as I decorate my tree. There is a Santa in an English walnut bed and a very pretty snowman made of felt and pompoms. Edna made a small Christmas stocking and one time a pretty napkin holder. I think of those crooked hands, and how it must have hurt, but she wanted to show her appreciation. Thank you, Esther!

Esther always felt sorry for Deana because she felt she was cheated because of her health. But Deana can rejoice in the love of her parents for her and for each other. Not many children have the heritage of unselfish love shown by her parents.

Esther tells the story of being at Northlake Mall and seeing this family of an old woman, a young man, and a little girl coming toward them. As she got nearer, she realized it was her family, and she was the old woman in the mirror. She burst into tears and wondered how Joel could love her. She also felt sorry for the little girl, Deana.

After renewing my memories of the Joel Smith family, I want to praise and thank my Lord Jesus for His salvation and His love, mercy, and goodness to my family and me. I have been blessed with good health, good friends, and two good husbands. Esther and I both came from large families. I loved meeting her family. She used to tell me about them and her early life. I was Edna Smith before I married, and I was delighted to learn that her mother-in-law was Edna Smith! Thanks for the memories, Esther, and may God bless you and yours!

Edna Bryan Reeves, who now lives in the Blue Ridge Mountains with her husband, is one of the original committee members.

Blessed By a Suffering Saint

Carolyn E. Hendricks

It was in the early 1970s when I first met Mary Esther when she came to Lilburn First Baptist Church. She was Women's Missionary Union Director and was very energetic and enthusiastic about her responsibilities as such. Since I had several very small children at home and kept four others' children, taught an active Sunday school class, and did some catering part time, I could not share her interest in WMU, but I respected her—even marveled at her. She became a member of my Sunday school class and was one of those believers with whom the Spirit connected with every lesson taught straight from the Word. All Sunday school teachers, who teach in His will, prepared for those kinds of members.

Mary Esther very much wanted a child, and when she became pregnant, she was PURE JOY walking! Soon after her daughter was born, she began having some health problems, which didn't seem serious at the time. But the symptoms progressed over a period of time, leaving her dependent on her husband and others. In years gone by, I've had many deep talks with Mary Esther about spiritual matters. She often requested prayer for others and was alarmed when sin prevailed in someone's life. The only request she made for herself was that she know and be able to accept

God's will for her life, even if it wasn't His will to have healing this side of glory. But I've never once heard her complain about her condition, her position that eventually led to a wheelchair. I began as the Teacher and have become the Learner. Countless others have been blessed by this Suffering Saint's life! Amen and amen!

In love and gratitude,
Carolyn

Carolyn Hendricks, an adult Bible study teacher at Lilburn First Baptist Church, is no stranger to suffering. Two of her six grandchildren have cystic fibrosis.

Blessed to Serve

Emmie Loften

I was working for Cornerstone Christian Bookstore when I met Esther. She actually came to a Bible study I had at my house with several others whom she knew very well—Amy Waters, Saundra Brewer, June Moloney, Phyllis Mann, who lived on her street, and others. Joel was so faithful to bring her, even though it was difficult even then to get her in and out of the car. Esther was very much into studying God's Word and into asking much in prayer.

When I began to help out with Esther, I was working at the bookstore and did not have to be there until 10:00 A.M. That gave me time to go help her get to the bathroom every morning after Joel left, and it meant that others did not have to come so early. We had time to read God's Word and pray together before I had to leave. I think the item we prayed for the most was our kids. We knew that without God's help, they would be lost to the world, and we wanted so very much to see them follow the Lord and be men and women who loved and honored God. Even many years after that, Esther would always ask, "How are Linda and Ricky?" I suspect those of us who helped Esther in the early stages of her illness were much more blessed by being able to serve her than she was by us, even though she needed our help very badly. I count it a great joy that God honored me in allowing me to serve her at that point in her life and in mine. God taught me to have compassion for the one who is hurting. For that I am grateful, Esther.

Emmie Loften, a neighbor of Esther's, is the manager of a Christian bookstore.

All Around the Town
with Esther

Nadra Strickling

I met Esther at Frances Bowen's Bible Study class, probably in 1974, because that's when we moved here from Greensboro, North Carolina. We were both members of Lilburn First Baptist Church at the time. My three children were all in school, one in elementary, one in middle school, and one in high school. Deana was in four-year-old kindergarten at our church. Esther was always ready to go somewhere and do something, so soon I was calling her almost every day to go places with me. After Joel left for work, Esther would get her house all clean for the day, and when I'd call, she'd say, "How soon can you be here?" She never said no!

On sunny days I would say, "Oh, Esther, it's too pretty to stay inside! Let's go somewhere today," and on dreary days, I'd say, "Oh, Esther, it's too nasty to stay at home. Let's get out of the house!" So for about two years, excluding the summers when my children were home and I took care of my two nephews, we went out every day, Monday through Friday.

I was and still am a "yard freak," and I must have dragged Esther to every plant nursery in town. We used to drive up to Lawrenceville to Cooper's Feed and Seed to buy big bags of manure! Esther liked to plant things in her yard too, but for every ten plants I bought, she would buy one. I would get her to help me plant my flowers, and then we would go plant hers. She was a little stiff and sore in those days, and I used to tell her, "Come on, Esther, bending and moving will make you feel better." And so she did. I'm not sure Joel liked all the flowers we planted. They just got in the way of his lawn mowing. When we planted some holly bushes in her yard, we were worried that Joel would run over them with the lawn mower! Esther and Joel had a big vegetable garden for all the years they lived on Greenwood Drive. Toward the end of that time, Esther couldn't shell the peas anymore because of the arthritis, and she used to give them away to Janet Bowers. When they moved to King David Drive, they gave up the garden, because Esther wasn't able to process the vegetables anymore.

My motto has always been, "Don't stay home and be bored by yourself. Call up a friend and go out and be bored together!" I always called Esther at nine o'clock in the morning. She never called me first, because she was busy getting her house cleaned so she could go when I called. Sometimes I went over and dressed Deana, just because she was little and cute, and I liked to do it. We had to be back from wherever we went by noon to pick up Deana at kindergarten. Then we would usually go out to Burger King or some other place and get lunch. I split a lot of hamburgers with Deana, because at the time, I was skinny and didn't eat much! After lunch, we might go to the mall or other stores, but we had to be at my house when my children got home from school. Esther got home in time to cook Joel's supper. Sometimes, if I had something at my house already cooked, she would take it and pretend to Joel that she'd been home cooking all day! (Of course, he knew she was kidding.) "Oh, honey, this is so good!" he would say. We spent a lot of time harassing Joel. He says we were always together, and we were.

I never thought about there being anything wrong with Esther. I knew she had arthritis, but it didn't slow her down much, and we just did things together because it was fun. I needed her friendship as much as she needed mine. Sometimes she drove me around on our daily adventures, but as time went on, she became more tired, and I did most of the driving. She drove a big Ford Fairlane. When she got to the place where she couldn't drive it anymore, she and Joel sold the car to my son Gene, who was in high school at the time. He could pile all his friends in that big clunker! He got rear-ended several times, but no one ever got hurt because that big old car was so sturdy! When he went to college, we sold it to another student, so that car went through another generation of high school students!

Esther told me a funny story about a time she was driving down the road in Lilburn and there was a policeman following her in the police car. She was worried that he was going to give her a ticket and was watching him in her rear view mirror. She was so preoccupied with the police car behind her that she hit the car in front of her! Esther told the policeman, "I couldn't drive with you watching me," and he was nice enough not to give her a ticket!

Esther always used to tell me how handsome Joel was. She said he was the best-looking man she had ever seen! She married him after only knowing him a month. She sure picked a winner, because look at how faithful he has been all these years.

My daughter, Katrina, was married in 1981, and Esther was determined to come to the wedding. This was no small feat, as we had a backyard wedding at our house, and the area where the wedding took place was at the bottom of an embankment. There were stone steps down the hill. By this time, Esther was in a wheelchair, but that didn't stop her. She said that even if she had to roll down the hill by herself, she was going to be there! Joel and Bruce Coker carried her down the hill in her wheelchair.

After Esther moved to King David Drive, she was farther away from me, and at the same time my mother in Alabama started having problems with Alzheimer's disease. I had to go over there and spend weeks at a time taking care of her. Other people began to come and help Esther. There was one time after Esther and Joel had started going to Lilburn Alliance Church that both her church and mine were supplying meals for the Smiths. Esther had been to a clinic where they determined that she had to be on a special diet. Lilburn First Baptist was responsible for lunches, and Lilburn Alliance took dinners. I was one of the First Baptist people who took food over for several months.

Esther tells this story about me that I don't even remember. She says that one day she was all alone at home. Joel had forgotten to leave her lunch out where she could reach it, and because of the arthritis she couldn't get to the food. She just kept drinking coffee all day long and praying to God. At this time in our Christian walk, we were learning that we could pray for anything and that nothing was too small for God to be interested in. She was so discouraged and scared, she asked God to do something to assure her that He had not forgotten her. A beautiful red cardinal appeared at her window and sat on her windowsill for a long time. She knew that God had sent this bird as an answer to her prayer. Then the phone rang, and it was me calling to say that I had two hot dogs and was wondering if she wanted one. I went over with the hot dogs and in this way her prayers were answered. I don't know if she told me about the cardinal at the time. I don't remember. But she knows that those hot dogs were God's provision for her that day.

I've been working for the last twenty or so years, and I haven't been involved in Esther's care during that time. But now we've reconnected because of this book. I have moved to a house that is wheelchair accessible, and we are going to get together. I'll be bringing her flowers out of my yard again!

Nadra Strickling is a member and children's teacher at Colonial Woods Baptist Church in Lilburn. She, along with three partners, owns a tax and accounting business. She and her husband Jimmy are parents of three adult children and six grandchildren.

One of the Original Five

Susan Coker

I met Esther at Lilburn First Baptist Church in about March, 1974. I had only come to know the Lord about two months earlier, and I was very excited about my newfound faith but was very shy about going to church. I felt like I must surely have a big, scarlet "S" for "Sinner" branded on my forehead, and that everyone there must know that I was returning to church after many sinful years of absence. I slid into a Sunday school class, trying to be as unnoticeable as possible. However, Esther noticed me. She set out to befriend me, to make me feel welcome, to dispel all my feelings of being an outsider. Esther called me at home, invited me to a prayer group led by Frances Bowen, and insisted that I come. I went to this and many others. Esther was always there making me feel included.

Esther was a little stooped then, and she told me she had arthritis, but I never knew she was in any pain. She always had a big smile on her face. Deana was about two years old then, and I remember that she would only eat cheese, nothing else! One time Esther and Deana drove over to my house, and I noticed how her knees were bent, but she was still walking and still smiling. I never knew anyone with severe arthritis before, and I didn't realize what was happening to Esther. In those early days, one of Esther's good friends from Lilburn First Baptist Church was Nadra Strickling. She recognized Esther's needs before anyone else did, and she came regularly to help her and do things with her.

According to my old calendars, I started going over to help Esther in 1979, taking her to doctors and on other errands. At the time, I was helping out with our church's senior citizens club, "Happy Agers." I took Esther with me often, where we did crafts and ate wonderful potluck lunches brought by the Lilburn locals twice a month. It got her out of the house, and she was good company for the older ladies.

I have a vegetable garden, and one spring I decided I wanted some fresh manure to add to the soil. After getting permission from the person who owned the cow pasture, I picked up Esther one day, and we drove out to Snellville. At that point, Esther was still walking with assistance, but had to sit on a stool because her knees wouldn't bend to allow her to sit down. I had my fold-up stool in the trunk of the car, my black plastic bags for the manure, and a shovel. Esther sat on the stool in the cow pasture and supervised my shoveling manure into the bags. It turned out to be a more strenuous job than I had imagined, and I was very tired when we got back!

The next thing I remember was when Esther was at Emory University Rehab Center, where she was recuperating from hip and knee replacement surgery in both hips and knees, originally done at DeKalb General Hospital. Joel said this was in 1981. One of the hips never would heal, so the doctors removed all the metal parts and left her with no hip. Joel says that is the one part of her body that bothers her the least! I went down to see her several times, and she walked out on the patio with crutches and braces on her legs. I think I must have pushed her in a wheelchair to the patio. She was there for weeks; I've forgotten how long. Joel's mother was taking care of Deana during the day, and Joel kept her at night. When she got out, she went to her mother-in-law's house to recuperate for a while. I visited her once, and she was still smiling. I still didn't realize how handicapped she was. While Esther was in the Rehab Center, Joel sold their split-level house on Greenwood Drive and bought a ranch-style home on King David Drive, less than a mile from my house. Prior to all those surgeries, Esther was at Emory Rehab Center, where the physical therapists were trying to straighten her legs. That was a painful and futile effort, but Esther was a survivor.

After Esther returned home, her Spanish friend, Beatrice, found her a housekeeper and helper. She was Elvia Esperanza, a young girl from Colombia, South America, who had a two-year old little girl named Luz and who needed a place to live. Elvia lived with the Smiths for about a year and a half, helping to take care of Esther, keep house, cook, and look after Deana and her own daughter. That was an ideal situation for both Elvia and Esther. While Elvia helped Esther with her physical needs, Esther helped Elvia with her English. Unfortunately, the Smiths found out that the Department of Immigration was looking for Elvia because she was an illegal immigrant, which they had not known. Elvia had to leave suddenly and go into hiding from the Immigration Police! She later married and moved to Chamblee, but she and Esther stay in touch with each other by telephone.

I was always looking for some way to help Esther, hoping that whatever we did would help her to get better. So on Thursdays I picked her up, and we went to the DeKalb YMCA to water aerobics classes. Saundra Brewer took her on Mondays. I had to help her get out of the wheelchair and into a swimsuit. Then she walked with her crutches to the side of the pool. There was an apparatus there, like a giant swing that lowered her into the pool. I jumped in, and we exercised together with all the senior citizens! (We were young things then. Now *we* are the senior citizens!) Then it was back to the dressing room and on to a restaurant for lunch. We had worked up an appetite, and we always pigged out! Esther could eat as much as I did, and sadly, that was a lot!

One day, I was so surprised when she called me up crying and saying that she couldn't get out of bed. I jumped in my car and drove over. I didn't realize what had been happening to her. It seems that on Mondays and Thursdays when she went out to water aerobics with Saundra and me, she ate big meals. But on the other days that she stayed home, she couldn't open the containers in the refrigerator because her hands hurt, so she ate nothing for lunch. Somehow her mind told her body she wasn't hungry, so she didn't even eat much supper, which Joel fixed at night. Because of this, she had gotten herself into a state of severe malnutrition. About the same time, we heard about the Hammer Clinic, a group of chiropractors who specialized in nutrition. She had an appointment with them, and they put her on a special diet to build her body up again. I remember that Joel stopped at the health food store every day after work and brought home fresh-squeezed carrot juice for her to drink. After a couple of months of intensive nutritional therapy, she regained her strength. At some time during that period, people from both Lilburn First Baptist and Lilburn Alliance Churches were bringing dinner to the Smiths every night for several months. God has blessed them with so many friends to help!

I lose track of chronology, but some time during that period, Esther went to the Southeast Chronic Disease Center in North Carolina for a month. The doctors there took her off all food for ten days, totally fasting her and cleaning out her system. Then they added back one food at a time, trying to find out if she was allergic to any foods. Shellfish was one of the culprits, also apples, corn, and even plastics. She could not wear anything but cotton, as polyester material caused her skin to break out. We used to say that Esther was our "canary in the mines" because whatever environmental pollutant or food additive that might be only slightly harmful to us caused Esther to break out in psoriasis. Joel worked hard to stick to those special diets from the Hammer Clinic and the Chronic Disease Center to help her nutritionally. Also, Deana was growing up and starting to help cook suppers. She would come home from school and jump right in taking care of her mother and doing the cooking and housework. Esther would tell her step-by-step what to do in the kitchen, and at age eight or so, she was preparing meals. My boys were still out riding their bikes and playing in the dirt at her age. Deana did this all the years she was home. We wondered what on earth Esther would do when Deana went off to college, but the Lord supplied helpers when the time came.

Another "bonding" experience between Esther and I was when she was seeing Dr. Robert McClure, the dermatologist, for her psoriasis. For some reason, she had to have her blood checked at regular intervals during her treatment. Since I had been a medical technologist some years before, I knew how to stick fingers and make a blood smear. Dr. McClure let me do this for Esther at home, saving her a trip to his office. Emmy Loften was working at his office, so I would take the slides to her there.

Esther always took everything like a trooper. She never let us know if she was discouraged or hurting. She knew that if she complained all the time about how she felt, no one would want to be around her! Knowing that and being able to do it are two different things, but Esther always managed to be cheerful and caring. She rarely let us know how bad she was feeling and always showed an interest in our families and us.

I have always told her that no matter how badly I may feel physically for whatever reason, I can never feel sorry for myself because of her example! I have one arthritic finger, and every time I look at it and wish it weren't so crooked, I think of Esther. I thank God that it's the only place in my body where I have arthritis. It serves as a reminder to pray for Esther. She has always been so brave and so able to keep her pain to herself around her friends. Joel has been the one to hear the part she kept hidden from us. Who can say how much pain he has experienced in watching his precious wife suffer, all the while selflessly caring for her for so many years? We all know he will have many jewels in his crown in Heaven, as will Esther and Deana.

There came a time when some of us realized that Esther couldn't stay home alone anymore. Saundra and I and three other ladies (Edna Bryan Reeves, Frances Holland, and I don't remember the other one, maybe Lynette Bachman) took one day a week to come over, help her get dressed, and stay with her for the day while our kids were in school. Each of us had a different "ministry" to Esther. Mine was shopping! We got in the car and went all over town! Getting in the car was a chore in itself, but we always managed. Once when I had had knee surgery and couldn't bend my knee for a couple days, I realized how hard it was for Esther to get in the car because she couldn't bend her knees. We went to the malls, the health food stores, grocery stores, doctor's appointments, Bible studies, everywhere. Other friends helped by cleaning or doing the wash. Esther has had several friends over the years who have decorated her house, wall-papered, made and hung curtains, and painted. Joel's talented mother was always making something beautiful to go in her house. Some people liked to cook. I loved to go over there on the days Anne Shriver was there and dine on her gourmet Italian delicacies! Emmie Loften, who lived nearby, came over every morning for two or three years and read the Bible to Esther before she went to work in the Christian bookstore. For many years, there were mainly the five of us. Then I think it was when I started back to school at Georgia State, and started substituting in the schools in 1984, that Saundra and Edna convinced enough people at Lilburn Alliance Church that there needed to be more people involved. The "Esther Committee" was established.

Now there were about twenty people who took one day a month to come and stay with Esther, and I was one of them. Again, each of these ladies brought their own special way of ministering to her. However, it is important to realize that while each of us was taking care of Esther physically, she was ministering to us all with her friendship, love, and deep spiritual understanding. Many are the days I went over there, hurting and angry about things that were going on in my life. After being with Esther all day, analyzing my feelings, applying the Word to the situations, and praying together, I came away feeling better. She did this with everyone who came over to help.

In 1983, Esther was chosen by the Goodwill Industries to be one of three people in the Atlanta area to receive a free home study course in computer programming from Control Data Corporation. That was before most of us knew anything about computers. I remember wondering what she was talking about, "needing another phone line for the computer!" It was to be a four-to-six month course, but it took her a year and a half because of the replacement surgery and recuperation time, which interrupted her study. She finished the course, and Goodwill tried to find her a job. They took her on several field trips and interviews, but in those days, there was not much work to be done from the home. Esther had no way to get to a job, so nothing ever came of it. There was a period of several years when she did telephone research polls from home. I remember taking her one time to turn in the results of her work to the lady who was in charge of the projects. That was a good job for Esther because she loved to talk on the phone! She had to give it up when her hands got so arthritic that she couldn't write.

I volunteered to teach Deana to drive when she was sixteen years old. Joel didn't have time when he got home from work, and I was an old pro at it, having just taught my two sons to drive. I remember the day Esther and I took her to get her driver's license. We were all nervous wrecks, but she passed. Deana and I really bonded through that experience, and we remain good friends today. I kept her resumé on my computer for years, so whenever she needed to change jobs, she came over and we had a "resumé party." Now she is all grown up and does her own resumés. Deana also was my "housekeeper" for about three years from about age fifteen until she went to college. After my sons had their drivers' licenses and got jobs outside the home, I lost my house cleaners. Deana took over the job of dusting and vacuuming for me on every other Saturday. I knew she had been singing in church, and one day I asked her to sing for me. Standing by my piano, dust rag in hand, she sang "On Holy Ground," with the voice of an angel. Every time I hear that song, I think of her.

Deana had only one car wreck. Lynette and her husband Rick had given her a car. She got hit on Highway 29 in Lilburn, and just to show God's providence, her car spun around and landed in the parking lot of the Christian bookstore! This reminds me of the fact that all the years Deana was growing up, she never lacked for anything. Esther's medical bills have always been astronomical, so God provided for her through others. Joel's mother made her beautiful dresses. Friends met their every need. One day after church, the Smiths found a brand new set of encyclopedias in the back of their van. I don't think they ever found out who gave it to them.

There was a time in my life when the Lord used Esther to minister to me more than ever. I was in Mississippi after my father had broken his hip in the fall of 1988. I was attempting to help my parents move out of their house and into a retirement home in the next city. I had not slept in three nights, and my nerves were absolutely shattered. I was desperately seeking God on my knees when the phone rang. It was Esther calling long distance from Lilburn. I have never had such an instantly answered prayer! It was like a voice from Heaven. At that time, I was so alone and burdened with anxiety and fear, I knew for the first time what it was like to be in serious emotional need. After talking with Esther, I went back to my knees and told God that I would never hesitate when she called me again. I promised I would drop whatever I was doing to go to her, because He had shown me through that experience what Esther must have been feeling all these years. She had a desperate need for her friends.

After returning home, I went into clinical depression and was very sick for a year. I finally went to a psychiatrist after not getting any better in six months, and between the medicine and the prayers of my friends, I recovered. But during that year, Esther played a big part in my emotional hanging-on. My father had given me some money to change Esther's bathroom around and to buy a special bath-giving apparatus from the handicapped supply store. Since there was someone assigned to be at Esther's every day, I went over twice a week, and we had "bath parties." It took two of us to operate the equipment and get Esther in the tub. We sat around and talked in the bathroom while Esther lay in the bathtub with the portable whirlpool hanging over the side of the tub and churning away. We had more fellowship in that bathroom than anybody could ever need!

The depression would only leave me when I was in the presence of Christian friends, and so those hours in the bathroom were how I got through the day. We talked about our problems, talked about the Lord, and generally had a grand time! Then we would eat lunch together. Sometimes I stayed until 3:00! I tell Esther that everyone in Lilburn has seen her naked! She handles it a lot better than I could! When I got a job as a parapro in December 1989, the bath parties ended. For some reason, no one else felt led to continue the bath ministry. I hated that, because those baths really made her feel better for a couple of days afterwards. Later, the Lord showed me that the relief from my depression came because He was present in the lives of Esther and her friends, and therefore I was in *His* presence when I was with them.

It was in March of 1997 that Esther became so sick that she had to go into the hospital again. She was at Northside Hospital for six weeks. We all thought we were going to lose her. She had congestive heart failure, the diabetes was out of control, and of course, the ever-present psoriasis was kicking in. She was on life support systems for days. The doctors told her that they couldn't keep on sustaining her life that way, and that at some point, they would have to take her off all the machines. If her body didn't take over, she'd be gone. One day I was visiting at the hospital when Deana was there. Esther was asleep, and we didn't want to disturb her. Deana and I sat on the floor crying and talking about losing her. But it wasn't the Lord's time for her, and when they unplugged the machines, Esther came back to life! Of course, that was just one of many times that Esther was in the hospital. Joel says she averages between thirty and seventy days a year in the hospital, usually for the arthritis. To further complicate things, the psoriasis always flares up whenever she gets any kind of infection or acute arthritic episode.

At that point, Esther's health was so fragile that the church ladies felt they weren't qualified to take care of her at home anymore. She was also bedridden, and many of the ladies were not strong enough to take care of Esther's needs. She no longer had the strength to do her part in moving herself around.

At last, government agencies recognized her need, and sitters were authorized to come to stay with her. Esther had a succession of sitters, but she also spent much time alone in the bed or in the wheelchair, totally dependent on the Lord to take care of her, as she could not get up by herself. Joel's work schedule has not often coordinated with the schedules of either the church ladies or the sitters, so Esther has spent many hours by herself. However, the Lord has always been faithful, and whenever she needed something, someone would call or show up. I have been the "Emergency Potty Person" ever since I went back to work in 1989. Since I live close, I can hop in the car and be there in five minutes. I never regret interrupting supper or anything else I may be doing, because I will never forget that moment in Mississippi when the Lord used Esther to answer my desperate prayer, and I made that promise to Him. It is also true, though, that no matter when I go over to help Esther, I always come away blessed by being with her. We laugh and say we would have never known each other so well if she hadn't been sick. That's true for all of us who have helped Esther. She is like the hub of a wheel of friends who have gotten to know each other over the years because of her. Her annual Christmas luncheons are like reunions of old friends, plus the always-widening circle of new friends she makes each year.

In 1998, Esther fell in the bathroom and broke her arm. She was then unable to use her forearm crutches and therefore unable to walk. Not long after that, one of her sitters was improperly handling her in her wheelchair, and her kneecap broke. Since then she has not been able to walk, but Esther has never lost her spunk, her joy, or her interest in other people. She is happiest when she is surrounded by people.

Esther is an inspiration to know; someone who has had more troubles than Job, but who has never lost her faith in God or her love for people. God has rewarded her with many friends. We used to spend many hours analyzing why God hasn't healed her. Both of us finally grew to accept the fact that we will never know why God does what He does, and we must accept His will for our lives whether we like it or not. When we can do that, we can have that peace that passes understanding, and joy in the midst of our circumstances. Knowing Esther has been a continuing spiritual lesson for me, one that I won't completely understand until I get to Heaven and ask our Lord to explain. I know one thing: He has shown His mercy, His grace, and His power through Esther and Joel's lives in a way that I might never have seen. Watching the way they live in total dependence on Him and witnessing His faithful care of them has been a faith-builder for me. I am greatly in their debt for their being the sacrificial lamb for my edification.

Susan Coker, long-time friend of Esther's, sings in the choir and teaches Sunday school at Atlanta First Baptist Church. She is a Special Education paraprofessional at Lawrenceville Elementary School.

How the Learner
Became the Teacher

Frances Bowen

I remember the first time I saw Esther. She was all smiles, and I could see that she not only loved life, but she embraced life. Someone had told me that she had a very bad case of arthritis, so when I met her, I expected to see a person who had constant pain showing on her face. That was not the case with Esther. She never complained. She was always enthusiastic about getting out and about and was all smiles, which made a lasting impression on me.

Esther loves the Lord. She loves to share Him and invite people to experience the same closeness with Him that she has. I was leading a home Bible study in 1974, and Esther was always inviting people to come to the study. Not long after I met her, she began to have to stay at home more and more.

I really saw the character of Esther in the way that she accepted her arthritis. One day she explained to us how long it took her to get out of bed. She explained that she had to move one area of her body at a time to limber the joints so that they would move together. She would stay in the bed and begin to move fingers first, and then arms, and later her legs. She said many times she would have to roll out of bed, and it would then take her twenty to thirty minutes to be able to move any farther. She shared the pain she experienced just to be able to brush her teeth. To think of a person having to go to all this trouble just to get up and out of bed was truly an inspiration to me. I think most people would have been tempted to give up after experiencing that much pain, say "It isn't worth it," and stay in bed permanently. I saw in Esther a radiance of love and acceptance. I never heard her question why she had this disease and never heard her ask, "Why me?" She was so appreciative of all that was done for her. She has truly been an inspiration to me because she exhibits the qualities of the fruit of the Spirit. All those attributes I saw radiate from Esther. For me, she became the teacher, a living example of what I could only try to teach.

Frances Bowen, Bible teacher and clerk at an elementary school, was one of the earliest influences on Esther's spiritual journey.

Conforming to the Likeness of Jesus

Martha Nunnally

I met Esther in a Young Married Women's Sunday school class at Lilburn First Baptist Church about twenty-eight years ago. She received the diagnosis of rheumatoid arthritis soon after that, and we prayed for her, never dreaming what havoc that disease would wreak in her body. I watched her go from a very happy, active wife and mother to a person confined to her bed most of the time, not happy about her circumstances, but with great joy from the Lord. One thing that stands out in my mind about Esther is her sweet smile, which I love!

Esther has great discernment, and the Lord has used these years of confinement to bring many people to her to unload their problems. This happens when they come to "help" her. The Lord has given her a lot of wisdom and has used her in ways she probably doesn't realize. She has meant a lot to me through the years, even though circumstances have kept me from spending a lot of time with her these past several years.

Esther has been an example to many of us that God can use life's hardest trials to conform us into the likeness of His Son, Jesus Christ, if we have trusted Him as our Savior. Time after time, I have seen Esther's strong will and determination finally melt before the Lord as she has given it to Him and has allowed Him to do His perfect work in her.

Martha Nunnally is a member of Lilburn Alliance Church. Her children are grown, and she works for Ronald Blue (financial consultants).

The "Earthly Hound" Used by the Hound of Heaven

Janet Bowers

I started going to Lilburn First Baptist in late August of 1970. Esther was one of two people who really made a very large and important impression on the "pre-Christian" (who thought she was a real Christian) that I was back then. First there was Gene Allen, who showed me to the nursery where I was to leave five-month-old Douglas during services. Then there was Esther, whose Sunday school class I joined a short time later. I think that is where I met her, but my memory train has jumped its track about the exact time and place. She always seemed to be there, smiling and making certain that I knew all about what the church had to offer, and talking to me in the pew before the service started. To a very reserved Yankee, who had been brought up to think that you do not talk the minute you enter the sanctuary, this venerable Southern practice of visiting before the meeting was the height of discourtesy to God!

Then Jesus drew me into His loving arms and saved me during the Christmas season of 1970. After that, Esther's friendliness and talking about the Lord all the time made perfect sense. That fall, she introduced me to virtually every woman in Lilburn First Baptist. Those women were to become my mentors in the Christian life. They taught me how to walk with the Lord and serve Him. Esther, with her dynamic personality coupled with a ready wit, lovingly dragged an overwhelmed, shy "new Southerner" to a multitude of baby showers, wedding showers, circle meetings, and Bible studies that ultimately led to my salvation. Who could stand against such love? Not me! I later read the poem, "The Hound of Heaven," and then I knew just who had been after me all that time. He was just using Esther.

She took me to a Bible study in Norma Fleming's home and introduced me to Grace Moore, who instilled in me a love of God's Word that abides to this day. Esther and I went together until she had Deana and then became so ill. She and I were diagnosed with different forms of arthritis the same week and announced our plights at a circle meeting. I'll never know why she was struck so viciously with the form that she has, and I was touched so lightly in comparison. But never once did she ever belittle my pain or play the "my pain is greater than your pain" game that some are so fond of doing. With her, all find an empathetic ear that understands that pain is pain, regardless of its magnitude.

Esther is a special person in Jesus' Kingdom—so unique that there will never be another like her. "I love you, Dear Heart! I owe you more than I can ever say. The times I have served you have been a pleasure."

Janet Bowers is a long-time neighbor and friend of Esther's. She has a beautiful singing voice and is a very talented seamstress and drapery maker.

Many Good Times

Frances Holland

We go a long, long way back, don't we, Esther? Deana was very, very small when I first met you. I believe you lived off Lawrenceville Highway at that time. Edna Bryan Reeves, our dear friend, called me one day and said she, Saundra Brewer, and Emmy Loften really needed someone to work with them in helping you out. That is when I really got to know you well, and very personally (ha, ha).

We had many good times talking and laughing together. We had good times praying for our families and friends together. And of course, there were the times of taking care of your needs and you ordering me around and telling me what to do (ha, ha). I remember the sponge baths and greasing you up with the creams and all the discomfort you had. As I said before, the laughter in doing it all made it more bearable. I would often push you out on the driveway so you could enjoy the fresh air and sunshine. I remember how excited you were to get your house redecorated, and how it helped to brighten your days. We rejoiced and thanked the Lord for all the blessings.

Soon other ladies started coming to assist you a few hours a week. This helped you out tremendously. We have had such good times at the Christmas luncheons that you,

Joel, and Deana prepared for all of us for so many years. I remember the love that went into all the preparation of those meals.

Esther, dear friend, you have been such an inspiration and blessing to so many people and especially to my family and me. I thank God for you and our special friendship. I love you, Esther.

Frances is a charter member of Lilburn Alliance Church. She has known Esther for twenty-eight years, has three grown girls, and lives in Lilburn.

Building Treasures in Heaven

June Moloney

Esther and I met through a mutual friend at Lilburn Alliance Church. She needed someone to come in one day a week and bring a meal. The first thing I noticed about Esther was her smile and love for the Lord. For someone who had been so active and now was dependent on the help of others, she was remarkably not bitter.

Once during a difficult time in my life, Esther shared a favorite Scripture:

> *The Lord is my light and my salvation—whom shall I fear? The Lord is the stronghold of my life—of whom shall I be afraid? When evil men advance against me to devour my flesh, when my enemies and my foes attack me, they will stumble and fall. Though an army besiege me, my heart will not fear; though war break out against me, even then will I be confident* (Psalm 27:1-3).

I'm sure she has many favorite passages, but this special one is what I needed to hear at the time and is marked in my Bible with Esther's name beside it.

One can't mention Esther without thinking of Joel. How many men remember the "in sickness and in health" part of the wedding vows? He carries out this promise with such love and patience.

We were part of a carpool that transported my two children, my sister's two, and Deana to Killian Hill Christian School for several years. Esther was always actively involved in Deana's homework and any school function in which she participated.

One day I received a call that someone who was responsible for helping Esther that day could not make it. They asked if I would fill in. Somehow I got a meal together, threw two kids and a bicycle in the station wagon, and drove the short distance to Esther's. Upon returning home two hours later, imagine my surprise to discover our house had been robbed! While I was "storing up treasures in Heaven," someone was swiping my microwave!

Esther's attitude in the midst of her many challenges has always been an inspiration to me. The days when it is difficult to function because of the "blahs" or the "blues," I think of Esther and give myself a swift kick in the "poor me!" I thank the good Lord I am able to do so much.

Over the years, people have come and gone in the lives of Esther and Joel. Other responsibilities may take someone away, but the Lord always provides someone else to take that person's place. I'm very thankful that I was one of the chosen.

June Moloney, a Lilburn neighbor, is one of Esther's long-time friends. She is married to Kevin and has two grown children.

Esther's Warm Smile

Jeri Hartman

She gave to me first the sweetest smile in the entire world and then the most understanding friendship of anyone.

I moved to the Lilburn area in 1977 and was visiting churches to find a new church home. I had just finished praying and asking the Lord if Lilburn Alliance was where I should be. I turned to leave after the service and Esther, who at that time used one crutch, was sitting on the back pew. She gave me the most precious, warm smile. I knew immediately that the Lord had put a special friend in my life path.

Through the years, we have laughed, cried, prayed, and grown closer in spirit. Sometimes we may go a couple of months without visiting, but we talk on the phone, and when we do see each other again, it is like we never missed a day. She has and continues to be a good, strong influence in my life and now in the life of my granddaughter, Holly. Her school class at Providence has adopted Joel and Esther, and now Esther has added more people to her prayer list.

There have been times when I wonder why Esther has to suffer so. I know I shouldn't, but I am human. Then God shows me the influence she has had on so many lives and the ripple effect. Still, I know that when we are in Heaven, we will *run* to greet each other!

Jeri Hartman, a grandmother and old friend of Esther's, attends Lilburn Alliance Church and lives in Stone Mountain, Georgia.

Esther's Example for Other Arthritis Sufferers

Jerry Lynne Waterworth

My first acquaintance of Esther and Joel began in St. Joseph's Hospital therapy pool about twenty years ago. I watched Esther being lowered into the pool as I went through my exercise routine with the other arthritis patients. We began conversing and realized that we were nearly neighbors—she being from Lilburn and I from Lawrenceville. I looked forward to my pool visits with Esther, and our friendship grew, as our girls became friends at Killian Hill Christian School. We attended Lilburn Alliance Church for a short time and enjoyed fellowshipping with Esther and Joel there. I have found Esther's faith to be a great encouragement to me as I have coped with my own rheumatoid arthritis. Her whole life has been a testimony of God's faithfulness.

The main difference between Esther's arthritis and mine is that my body has tolerated and responded to the medications while Esther's body has not. I have watched as Esther's body has withered and her faith has been made stronger. Truly His power is perfected in her weakness. We have remained friends over the years, and she is a marvel to my family. Joel's commitment to Esther has been a wonder to behold, and it has been a privilege to pray daily for them for many years. We love them both.

Jerry Lynne Waterworth, a fellow arthritis sufferer, lives in Dacula and attends Hebron Baptist Church.

*Joel and Esther celebrate a
wedding tradition*

Esther and Joel share a snack with the birds

*Esther shares a moment with her
daughter, Deana Marie*

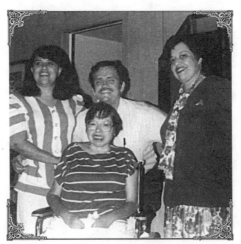

*Esther, Joel and her sisters,
Geraldine and Hope*

Esther with her friend, Edna Bryan Reeves at her wedding

Esther enjoys the warm waters of Haaii during Joel's R&R from Vietnam

A younger Joel, poses in
front of his base in California

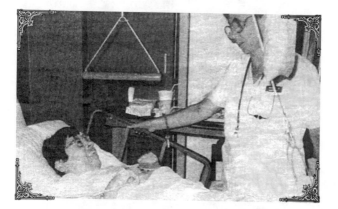

Esther Chatting with a Nurse
during one of her many
hospital stays

*Esther enjoys the company
of her guests at one of
her annual Christams luncheons*

*Esther and students from
Providence Christian Academy*

The Veterans

My Friend Esther

Lynette Bachman

My earliest memories of Esther go back to the end of 1981. We were both attending Lilburn Alliance Church, and I first noticed her and Joel in our Sunday school class. We were in the young married class, led by Jack and Nancy Stanton, located in the green trailer that sat out in the parking lot where Steinmann Hall is now. My husband Rick and I had just moved to Georgia from Southern California and immediately began the hunt for a new church home. We found Lilburn Alliance on the first try and have been there for twenty years.

The reason I noticed Esther right off was because she was using a special kind of arm crutches, which I had never seen before. She managed to climb the steps to the trailer with a little help. It looked like a normal way of life for her. I soon learned that Esther had been afflicted with rheumatoid arthritis for several years.

It was the next summer of 1982 that Edna (Bryan) Reeves told me that Esther needed help. She told me that Esther was unable to get out of bed by herself in the mornings, nor could she get herself cleaned up, so I said I would be willing to help out. I think I went over once a week for a short time until more ladies were found. Then I went over twice a month. In the later years, I cut back to once a month. In the beginning, I took along my three-year-old son, Eric. Esther loved having little children around. She always had coloring books, crayons, and puzzles. My son, though, usually just liked watching and listening while I worked with Esther.

My job consisted of getting Esther up to use the toilet, assisting her back to the bed to get a sponge bath, dressing her, putting her crutches on her arms, and leading her out to sit in her wheelchair. She asked me to make her some covers for her crutches so the arm rests wouldn't get so dirty. I made them out of washcloths with elastic to hold them on. After she was sitting comfortably in her chair, we would visit for a while. Then it would be time for lunch. I would bring a sack lunch for both of us to eat. She used to call it a picnic lunch. We always had a nice time visiting together. We each shared about what was going on in our lives. One thing about Esther is that she always holds confidences and she always prays for my family and me if we are having problems. As the years went by, we started feeling like a family.

Something that has always impressed me about Esther is that she has always taken part in any activity that was available if she could get to it. Whether she was feeling bad or not, she always made an effort to be at everything she could. The hardest part was getting her wheelchair up the steps at some of the ladies' houses, but we always found a way. Sometimes we wheeled her in through garages, back doors, up homemade ramps, and sometimes we carried her, wheelchair and all. One time we invited Esther and Joel over for dinner. We had just finished working on making our basement into rooms and Esther wanted to see it. Off we went, pushing the wheelchair down the street, up the neighbor's driveway, up the hill into our backyard, and into the boat door. We pushed her all around to see our fine job of carpentry.

One day, I decided to take her for a walk down her street on King David Drive. She has this little cement ramp coming out of her kitchen door. I tipped her up to get over the door jamb and when we went forward, I didn't think about the slope and almost dumped her out of her chair. We laughed, but I really don't think Esther thought it was so funny. I told her she needed to get a seatbelt. Well, we did have a nice walk on that pretty spring day and I sure did get my exercise.

I know Esther is a "take-charge person." She might be down in body, but she is up in spirit. Whenever there is something to be done, Esther is right there in the middle of it, coaching and making her wishes known. In things like preparing meals, cleaning, planning schedules and parties, Esther has always been involved.

Speaking of parties, Esther always wanted to show her gratitude to the ladies for helping her so much. She would throw a big Christmas party each year for all of us. Joel, Deana, and her mother-in-law, before she passed away, would fix all the food. She would bring out her Christmas china and set the tables really pretty. We always had such a nice Christmas feast. After they got their screened porch added on, we were able to have everyone sit together out there when the Christmas season turned out warm. It was always fun to see all the ladies who had helped out all year. I wouldn't know who they all were until that day. Esther would always pray before the meal. We could tell how much she appreciated her friends by her prayer. Fun and fellowship were had by all.

Faithfulness to the Lord is another strong characteristic in Esther. She almost always makes it to church. She loves worship and praise. One of the things she regrets the most is not being able to raise her hands in praise. Over the years, I never have heard her complain about her lot in life. She has always been pleasant to be around and is an encouragement to me because she shows the Lord's strength in her weakness.

I also want to add that Esther could not have chosen a better man than Joel to be her husband. They have loved each other with the greatest love through sickness and health. Joel treats Esther like a princess. Esther told me that her mother named her Mary after the mother of Jesus and Esther after the queen of the Hebrews. She has certainly brought honor to those names. Joel has always been there for her through every situation. I respect him very much for his faithfulness to Esther every day of their lives.

I remember when Esther's gray cat disappeared. She was so disappointed and sad. Then one day, her daughter Deana brought home a little white kitten. They named it Snowy. It had crossed eyes and a broken, crooked tail. Esther fell in love with it immediately. She related with it because it was broken just like her.

At the end of 1999, we got the idea that Esther needed some stretching exercises every day to limber up her bones and joints. We gathered together a few ladies who said they would come over and work with her in that way. I would take over my vibrator to use on her neck and arms. Joyanna Blake taught us how to stretch her muscles very gently. We don't do it very often now, though, because it seems to hurt too much. I still go over most Fridays to talk to her and rub her neck and arms. I think it eases her stiffness a little.

The most important lesson I have learned from Esther is never to give up. I am sure God has spoken words of encouragement to her many times saying, "Hang in there." Esther has hung in there! Because I see that she can do that, I see that I can do that also. Whenever problems come to me, I can listen carefully to what the Lord has to say to me, be obedient to do what He says to do, and I can "hang in there" too. What peace of mind and joy we have knowing the Lord. *"The joy of the Lord is my strength"* (Nehemiah 8:10).

I remember many times when I have prayed for Esther to get well, but one time in particular stands out. We were at a Sunday evening church service. The pastor, Ken Whisenant, had a special prayer time for those who wanted healing. Joel pushed Esther down the aisle. They usually sat in the back of the church near the middle aisle so they could get out quickly if they needed to. When I saw them go forward, I immediately started praying. In fact, I started begging and crying for God to work a miracle in Esther's body, her legs in particular. I knew it would have to be a miracle because she had told me that she had had knee replacement surgery and the doctors messed up somehow. Plus, I knew that when she had undergone a hip replacement surgery, her body rejected the artificial hip and became infected. Following that surgery, Esther walked around minus a hip. How she ever did that I will never understand. She sure was a trooper. That night, I cried myself out praying for God's miracle for her, so she could walk again and God would be glorified. So far, the prayer has not been answered in the way we all wanted. A Bible verse comes to mind, *"God's ways are not our ways"* (Isaiah 55:9). I am sure God has a better plan. I do know that many ladies have been able to get out of themselves to help another. We have all received many blessings from being a part of Esther's life.

Lynette Bachman, originally from Southern California, is a mother of three grown children and attends Lilburn Alliance Church.

Esther the Queen

Karen Pollard

I have a friend I would like to tell you about. Her name
is Esther. It is interesting that her name is the same as
a famous queen in the Bible. You see, my friend Esther,
in my eyes, is very much a queen, and I'll explain why.

A queen deserves high value and respect. I respect my
friend, Esther, so much. She is disabled physically, but her
inner strength, rooted in a strong faith, shines every time I visit
her. She rarely has a "pity party," but more often than not,
when I come home from spending precious time with Esther,
I find that I have been blessed by her encouraging words to
me. I highly value my friendship with her because when I am
with her, we laugh, we cry, we share, we pray, we talk about
our families, our church, our common interests, and our concerns. How very proud I am to have Esther as a true friend.

Although her throne is a wheelchair, Esther has no
problem executing decisions and delegating responsibilities.
She is not timid and can ask for what she needs. I like that
about Esther. When I cut her hair, she tells me where to get
the towel that must be placed around her neck. (Esther does
not like tickly hairs on her face or neck, and I don't blame
her a bit!) She knows exactly how she wants it cut and
shaped, no wishy-washy timidity, just straightforward,
straight-talking, and real. When you spend time with Esther,

you know what she thinks and don't have to wonder where she stands on an issue! A very decisive queen, indeed.

Queens love a party, and my friend Esther is no different. Her favorite time of the year is Christmas, when she loves hosting a full-course, sit-down Christmas luncheon for her friends. I have had the privilege of attending her holiday parties many times, once with my mother who was visiting from out of state. I remember by mother marveling at the number of people she served. Each table was fully decorated and the food was exquisite, just like you would find at a queen's palace. Each of us leaves inspired and blessed with our tummies full. I will always treasure sweet memories of Christmas luncheons with my friend, Esther.

A queen is faithful to her kingdom and Esther is no different. Her king is Jesus, and His Kingdom and His Church are what she loves most. Her prayers, her faithful attendance, and her concern for her church family are an important part of Esther's life.

The pastor's family Christmas card photo remains on her refrigerator year-round, and she has a deep love for Lilburn Alliance Church. It is a love borne out of her personal relationship with the King of kings, her Lord and Savior, Jesus Christ. She provides a queenly example for all of us.

A crown? Surely every queen deserves a crown. I know that one day, my friend Esther will be given a glistening crown, not because she earned it, but because the Father will reward those who love and serve Him faithfully here on earth. My friend, Esther, is a faithful servant I choose to call a queen.

Karen Pollard, a member of Lilburn Alliance Church, has been a friend of the Smith family for fifteen years and provides haircuts for the family.

A Letter to Esther

Marjorie L. Magee

Dearest Esther,

I am thankful that I was able to be of help to you over the years before it became physically impossible for me to continue. I will be seventy-six in May, so I have definitely slowed down! I can remember the good times we had and the lunches we enjoyed together. I have a lot of good memories of the times we shared together, dear friend. I love you, Joel, and Deana. You are always in my prayers.

Lots of love,
Marge

Marjorie L. Magee, who resides in Duluth, Georgia, with her husband Bob, has a daughter named Kathy Ware, who is also a good friend of Esther's.

A Model of
Determination and Stamina

Kathy Ware

I have known Esther Smith for about fifteen years, and for most of those years when I was not working, I was involved in her life. For many years, I was on the schedule, along with other ladies, to make sure that Esther was taken care of every day. I usually visited her about once or twice a month. During our visits, I would take a lunch to share with her and her family. I would also give her a sponge bath and dress her. It was during the bathing that we would laugh a lot due to the awkwardness of the situation. I really appreciated Esther's sense of humor in making me feel comfortable.

One funny memory comes to mind as I reflect on our visits. I hate wearing shoes, so I took them off whenever I visited Esther. Imagine my surprise when Esther called me one evening to remind me that I had left my shoes at her house. I must have driven home barefoot!

Several times, I would take Esther to various places. It was always an ordeal getting her in and out of the car without dropping her. While I never did, I am sure that she endured a lot of pain with me hoisting, pushing, and pulling her. Yet she never complained. What a model of determination and stamina!

I am a single mother with two children, so a lot of responsibilities fall on my shoulders. When I am feeling sorry for myself because I have to mow the lawn, I remember how Esther would probably just love to take my place and be able to walk back and forth across my yard. In that way, Esther has helped me realize how lucky we are to be healthy, and my self-pity vanishes.

Kathy Ware, mother of two girls, has been a second grade teacher in Dekalb County for eleven years.

We Helped Each Other

Elvia Esperanza

I met Mrs. Esther in 1981 through a friend named Beatrice. I had come with my daughter, Luz, and her father from Colombia, South America, to find a better life and a better future for my daughter. I had a visa to go from Colombia to the Bahamas, and I went there in a small boat. Conditions were bad in the Bahamas for refugees. It was very hot, and people in the camp only received one meal a day and one bottle of water. I believe that God sent a guardian angel in the form of a man who had a small plane. He asked me if I wanted to fly to Miami, and of course I did. When we arrived at the airport, he told me to stay on the plane while he went inside. When he returned, he told me just to walk on through the crowds. No one questioned me or asked to see any papers. Later I found out that I could be in a bad situation if I was caught, because many people from Colombia were smuggling drugs into the country.

Mrs. Esther is a wonderful lady who opened her house to my daughter and me when I needed to work. I lived with them for about one year. In addition to needing to support my daughter and myself, I was able to send money back to my mother in Colombia, since she was very poor. Mrs. Esther gave me the opportunity to go to school to learn English. She arranged for a friend from her church to pick me up and take me back again twice a week for these lessons at a nearby church. Mrs. Esther's daughter, Deana, was about nine years old when I lived with the Smiths, and my daughter was about two years old. She loved Deana, and Deana loved her. I helped Mrs. Esther by sponge-bathing and dressing her each day, cooking, and keeping house for the family. Mrs. Esther loved the Spanish foods I cooked for her, and she taught me how to cook the American food that they liked.

Sadly, the Immigration Department found out about me, and I had to go into hiding quite suddenly. I felt very bad about leaving Mrs. Esther like that, with no one to help her. I was unable to work for a long time after that, but I did continue to baby-sit in my home.

I still go over to visit Mrs. Esther from time to time, and we talk on the phone. I will always appreciate that she helped me at the same time I was helping her.

Elvia Esperanza, now a United States citizen, works full time as a nanny for a doctor's family.

Gutsy Esther

Helen Barclay

I first met Esther when we moved to Lilburn in 1981. I had just become involved with the Pioneer Girls program at Lilburn Alliance Church, which we were attending. It was Christmas time, and we went to Esther's house to sing Christmas carols. I had not been around many handicapped people up to that time, and I was somewhat awed with the new experience.

Shortly after that meeting, the church called for volunteers to assist Esther each day in her home. A friend encouraged me to become involved, so I signed up to help once a month. I did myself a favor by doing this. Esther became my friend. I took courage from her positive spirit, her uplifting attitude, and her determination not to let her condition stop her from enjoying life. Esther always had a listening ear, and God blessed her with wisdom. It was a comfort to share our concerns together, and to pray for one another and our families. We enjoyed many lunches together, and when I moved to a new house, Esther was determined to come and visit. It took a big effort for her to do that, and I appreciated her interest and determination to see my new situation. That day we had lunch at *my* house.

Esther takes charge of her own household, using only the hands and feet of her helpers to keep her home as she wants it. I delight when she gets new things for her home, and it is always a pleasure for me to help her keep her home in order. I looked forward to the day in the month I would spend with her. Rarely have I heard Esther complain. When I first began to help her, she was determined to take a walk each afternoon on her crutches. We would walk together up the street about five houses and then back. That took twenty minutes or so. Esther, you are gutsy!

In the early days, Esther had a job using the phone, calling people for opinion polls. She had a desk/table set up in the family room, where each afternoon and evening she spent some time calling. It was a good job for a talented lady with wisdom and courage.

Another day Esther took to cleaning the bathroom basin all by herself—no help, thank you! And it was done! However, the cleaning agent turned out not to agree with her skin. Oh, well, better stick to the phone!

Her Christmas parties have always been a highlight of the season. Esther, we so enjoy coming to your house each year for our Christmas luncheon. We know it is a big effort for you, but you always do such a fine job of organization, and the food and tables are always outstanding. Thank you for honoring us, your helpers, in such grand style. We love you, Esther. You have enriched our lives with your wisdom, courage, and strength of character. Your love for Jesus is very evident. I'm glad you are my friend.

Helen Barclay, member of Lilburn Alliance Church, works for worldwide Christian apologist, Ravi Zacharias.

Fond Memories

Andi Worley

I think the thing I remember most about my days with Esther was the frequent shopping trips we took together. In the beginning, Esther was afraid to trust me to get her in and out of the car successfully. Gradually her confidence in me grew, and finally she came to the place where she looked forward to our going out each week. However, that didn't mean that she didn't find it necessary to instruct me on each step to take, from how to place her arms in her crutches to how to swing her around into the car. Each week she patiently explained this to me. You would think I might have learned the procedures after my years of being trained by her!

Those were the days when her daily companions came in and got her "cleaned, brushed, dressed, and ready to face the world." We always tried to hurry through this process on the days when she was able to go out. Usually our shopping trips began with lunch. Sometimes, if we had a lot of different stores to visit, we would just eat in the car. If not, we would venture into a restaurant—usually Chinese—that was one of her favorites. If there were any leftovers, and there usually were, they went home to Joel. He was never far from her thoughts. It always amazed me how she managed to take care of so many people from her wheelchair!

I don't know which of us enjoyed shopping more, Esther or me! Sometimes we just wandered through the stores, with me rolling her through the racks of clothes, and often as not, getting her wheelchair hung on one of the racks. Esther would suddenly disappear behind the clothing, and I would hear this voice saying, "Andi, watch out!" She always thought I rolled her a little too fast down the mall corridors. I guess I was more focused on getting from store "A" to store "B," and she was more focused on what she could see along the way! Our trips to the mall at Christmas time were always special.

We often had long conversations about colors and sizes, likes and dislikes. I admired Esther for her interest in clothing, colors and makeup, even though these were luxuries she couldn't often afford and would never have been able to use without assistance. She never accepted "just any old thing." She was avidly interested in what colors and styles of clothing Deana should wear. She selected items for Deana with the greatest of care and love.

Esther was the kind of friend with whom you had deeply spiritual conversations. If you had overheard some of these, you might have thought we were having Bible study, because she desired to know God's Word and how it applied to every area of her life. Esther and I have spent many hours just talking about the Scriptures and praying together. She prayed for my family and me, and I prayed for her and her family. Whenever she was feeling blue, I would try to go visit her and help her work through whatever was bothering her. But I was always uplifted by these times together because she had much to give as she shared about her love for her Lord and for her family. She was a good listener and a good counselor. But most of all, she was a good friend.

Esther's life is one of those rare ones that will keep on "making waves" on earth long after she has gone home to be with Jesus. Esther most often helped, in very meaningful ways, the women who came in to spend time helping her. I don't know many women who have had good health and more than adequate finances who have contributed as much to God's kingdom and to abundant living for His children here on earth as she has done. I am so grateful to God that I grew to know her as intimately as I did, and that the Lord allowed me to spend the amount of time with her that I was able to spend. What a special sister in the Lord she is! There are many here on this earth who "call her blessed."

Thank you, Esther, for being the woman of God that you are. I love you in Jesus!

Andi Worley, former member of Lilburn Alliance Church, is a ladies' Bible study leader and currently attends Atlanta First Baptist Church.

Esther the Intercessor

Dolly Mallory

In thinking back and contemplating the three years that I visited with Esther once a week, I am amazed at the "Amazing Grace" that she demonstrated in her life. Esther lived in a wheelchair and lived in constant pain, but she never complained. Her whole outlook on life came from the inner strength of her active faith in her Lord and Savior, Jesus Christ.

Esther and I had many opportunities to pray together. She always had others on her heart to pray for and to intercede on their behalf in their times of need. There is no higher calling in the Kingdom of God than exercising our priesthood through deep and abiding intercession. Esther fulfilled this calling daily in her life. It was my pleasure and privilege to sit with her and hear her heart for her family and friends.

Those were the years when Esther's daughter, Deana, was going through high school and looking forward to college. Esther's thoughts, energy, and prayers were always toward Deana for her future. She took such delight in her daughter and would bask in her accomplishments.

Esther was most appreciative of the help she received from her church family and friends. I have heartfelt memories of the Christmas luncheons she gave in honor of the many friends and helpers she had throughout the year. She was gracious to all. Esther's life shows forth the investment of her love and prayers in the lives of all who know her and have been recipients of her importation of the courage and grace of God.

Dolly Mallory is one of the associate pastors at Christ Fellowship Church. She is the pastor over corporate intercession and also serves as a pastoral counselor.

Who's Ministering to Whom?

Linda Smith

When I think back to my first introduction to Esther, I recall thinking *She is a sweet woman, but don't ask me to help her, Lord!* Out of guilt, I began going to Esther's once a month to minister to her. As time went on, I realized after each visit with Esther, she was actually ministering to me. I was a young, very inexperienced, and fearful mom. God used Esther in my life during this time. She spent countless hours in intercessory prayer for my family and me. She also encouraged me in my walk as a mom and with the Lord. The time each month with Esther was no longer a burden or done out of guilt, but became a time I looked forward to!

Then the Lord blessed us with a son. Unlike my daughter, I brought Aaron with me to Esther's each month. Esther so enjoyed talking to Aaron and even holding him. Aaron also learned not to fear people in wheelchairs or people who have handicaps. He felt the love and undivided attention he received from Esther, and it was priceless. He saw her as a whole person regardless of the wheelchair.

Esther had to endure with great patience a different woman coming to care for her each day of the month. We all did things differently. I know it was so humbling for

Esther to have to be bathed and dressed by each of us. But she handled it so graciously and patiently. She enjoyed the uniqueness that each of us had to offer.

I took over the scheduling for Esther and did it for about five years. The positive responses of those I called were such a blessing. There were times I faced opposition, but the Lord enabled me to do this ministry to His glory. At times I felt like giving up, but I would be reminded of what Esther faces just in everyday life, and it would give me the strength to continue on. The Lord taught me a lot during that time.

There were many times I transported her to the doctor or just out to get some lunch. We would both be worn out by the time we got home, but we always enjoyed doing it.

I remember an occasion when Vickie Williamson, our two young boys, and I took Esther to the park. We laughed so hard as the three of us struggled to get Esther in our van and then back out again. Sometimes the process went smoothly and other times it didn't. Esther always had a great sense of humor, which put us at ease. We all really enjoyed our day at the park.

Esther's annual Christmas dinners are a fond memory. She was always so excited to be blessing us with a dinner in our honor. The food was good and the fellowship was great. Deana and Joel were always such servants to enable her to have these dinners.

I don't even want to imagine what my life would have been like without knowing Esther. She showed me that true strength and perseverance come from the Lord, and with Him, we can walk through any valley or trial and come out victorious. Our lives on this earth are only a drop in the bucket compared to eternity. I look forward to spending eternity with Esther jumping and leaping and praising God!

Linda Smith is from Elkhart, Indiana. She now resides in Lawrenceville, Georgia, with her husband and two children.

Immediate Friendship

Vickie Williamson

I met Esther Smith in September 1988, at a ladies' Bible study at the Lilburn Alliance Church in Georgia. I recall seeing this very frail, wheelchair-bound woman across the room. Despite her obvious handicap, which I later learned was psoriatic arthritis, her face beamed. She seemed to be overflowing with joy. I was immediately drawn to Esther. Since my family had just moved from Massachusetts, I was eager to get to know her. Soon, a precious friendship blossomed. Even though I now live in New York, Esther remains one of my dearest friends.

Shortly after meeting Esther, I volunteered to be a part of a church ministry to help her for a full day every month. While I was assigned sundry tasks to help Esther, I was actually the one on the receiving end, benefiting from one blessing after another. Our discussions about our faith in Jesus and life in general will stay in my heart forever. Esther's wisdom and knowledge in the things of the Lord kept me looking forward to every moment I could spend with her.

I laughed more with Esther than anyone I know, sometimes to the point of tears. One time I unwittingly chose the hottest, most humid day of the year in "Hotlanta" to treat Esther and my kids at the zoo. People seemed so full of empathy that Esther had to endure the brutal heat. One woman, while we were in the ladies' room, actually displayed her disapproval, with eyes ablaze, that I had the audacity to put Esther through the misery. We laughed ourselves sick over that. Overall, what a trooper Esther was, barely able to breathe and with sticky wet clothes. She found humor in every aspect of that day.

As time went on, we hardly let a day go by without either talking on the phone or seeing each other. She knows me as well as any friend could know another. Once, I was going through a very difficult time, and I had not spoken to Esther about it. Esther called one morning and asked in a panicky voice what was wrong. I replied, somewhat puzzled, that nothing was wrong. She said, "Vickie, I know something terrible is the matter. Last night I awoke from a frightening dream. The Lord had me pray for two hours for you." The Lord called on Esther all right, because He knew He could count on her, His prayer warrior. Esther prayed for my children, my husband, and me all the time. I would love to know the number of hours she clocked in prayer on our behalf—and still does.

Esther genuinely loves my children as if they were her own. They recognize this, I am sure. I am also sure that Esther will have a lasting, godly impact on them. When my oldest son, Jamie, was about ten years old, he asked me how "Miss Esther" could smile all the time when she didn't feel well. No matter how many struggles Esther has had and will have, one thing is certain. She is filled with the love, peace, and joy of the Lord from head to toe. Esther's humility never ceases to amaze me. Her immobile condition necessitates aid from nurses or friends in all manner of daily living. Pride never gets in the way. She is at peace with whatever has to be done.

Is there any one particular thing that makes Esther so special? Is it the pure joy within her, despite the daily suffering? Is it that she gives her love so freely, willing to lay her life down even if it means sleepless nights? Is it that she has humility like that of Jesus? Is it her wonderful sense of humor that makes the worst of days bearable? Is it that she has a Scripture verse or godly wisdom ready for every problem or circumstance? Is it that Esther has a way of finding a rainbow around every corner?

Yes, it is all of the above!

A native of western Pennsylvania, Vickie Williamson, her husband Jim, and their three children now live in Poughkeepsie, New York.

A Fitting Tribute

Jack and Nancy Stanton

Esther, this is such a great opportunity to say we love you and to tell you what an encouragement you are to all those who come in contact with you. Your love of life shines through as well as your strength of character, your unfailing love for the Lord, and your faithfulness.

We have known you for many years; Deana was just a little girl when we met. We've seen so many treatments and life-threatening times, and still you have maintained your sense of humor, your love for others, and your deep love for the Lord. You are a wonderful example for all of us to follow.

Young couples can learn from you and Joel. You love each other, and you are steadfast no matter what circumstances you are in. Esther, you always enjoy having fun and having family and friends around. You take part and attend as many functions as you are able and love it. You show caring and friendship wherever you are. I remember a few years back when about six or seven of us met at your house for several weeks learning to do oil painting, and Betty Curl was our teacher. What a good time we all had! I remember how you would use your phone to contact people and pray with and for them. Life's lessons can be learned by your example. Young and old alike may glean knowledge and understanding. When we come to take care of your needs, instead of us blessing you, you give us a blessing we all cherish and keep in our hearts to this day.

You let God hold you in the palm of His hand; your trust is in Him. What a powerful statement that is, and one we all should follow. It is a pleasure to know you and your family, Esther. God has brought so many people into our lives that we cherish and hold dear. We praise Him for the friendships He allows us to have. You are a very special lady, not only in our eyes, but in God's as well. We love you, Esther.

Jack and Nancy Stanton are members of Lilburn Alliance Church, are retired, and have three grown children. They have been Sunday school teachers for over twenty years.

The Prayer Warrior

Judy Latrimore

As I begin to think and reflect on how Esther has touched and made an impact on my life, I immediately see, in my mind's eye, her wonderful, smiling face and the many times she has given me words of encouragement throughout the years. I've been privileged to know her.

I became one of "Esther's helpers" in the fall of 1985 and continued until we moved to Tennessee in 1996. When I began, Edna Reeves called for ladies who would commit to one day a month to minister to this special lady. At first I wondered if I could handle the various needs she would have. I will never forget when I went that first time. Being a little apprehensive, Esther told me that she had already prayed for me before I ever got there. What a word of reassurance that was for me! I'm sure that Esther prayed one by one for each lady as they came.

I guess the thing that stands out to me the most is Esther's steadfastness in prayer for others. I know, as I'm sure others do, that she cares for each of us and for our families. I'll be forever grateful for the many times she has interceded on our behalf, including times she helped me carry the burden of a wayward daughter. She gave timely words of encouragement and counsel, and we had countless good times of fun and fellowship.

I wasn't very brave when it came to taking Esther for a ride in the car, but on several occasions we did venture out. I think it might have appeared humorous to onlookers to note my awkward maneuvers to Esther's precise instructions. The fact that she was game to try still makes me smile.

To say she ministered to me far more than I ever did for her is an understatement. I credit Esther for helping to prepare me, in a sense, for the time I found myself having to care for my own mother for a short period of time.

Esther has been a precious part of my life, as well as a special blessing to my husband, Don, and our whole family. Truly she is one of God's special blessings. We love you, Esther!

Judy Larimore was a member of Lilburn Alliance Church when she met Esther. She now resides in the mountains of Turtletown, Tennessee.

A Good Listener

Alice Stancil

It is with the greatest pleasure that I take some time to focus on Esther Smith and how she has touched my life. The times I spent at her home helping with her care were so special. She knew me well. Esther truly knew how to listen. We shared prayer requests, and her faith helped me grow as a Christian. She is a powerful lady with a fighting spirit.

Esther's Christmas dinner parties were lovely, and everyone enjoyed the fellowship. I have been blessed by knowing Esther.

Alice Stancil is a long-time member of Lilburn Alliance Church and continues to be a blessing to others.

Esther's Lifelong Impact on Others

Anne Shriver

I was one of Esther's helpers for a period of about three and a half years back in the late 1980s and early 1990s. Knowing her made a lifetime impact on my children and me. I had prayed for two years for God to show me how He wanted me to help Esther, because I knew others were helping her and that more people were needed. My children were preschoolers at the time, and I didn't see how I could do anything. But eventually the Lord convicted me that I could take the children with me to help her, and that this would be a great witness to them in serving others.

My daughter, Rachel, who is now a senior in high school, was greatly influenced by those years spent helping Esther. It nourished in her a heart for serving others. In high school, she has been in ten different service clubs. She is receiving a $5,000 college scholarship as a service award. Seeing me bathe Esther made a big impression on her; she saw how Esther couldn't do anything for herself. As a result, she has had a heart for handicapped people. She once went on a mission trip to Mexico and served in a severely mentally and physically handicapped children's institution. She baby-sits for autistic and mentally retarded children. Our church has a soup kitchen after church, and Rachel feeds the children every week. She is considering becoming a pediatric physical therapist so she can make a career of helping the handicapped.

The first time I took my son, Philip, to church after he was born, I took him up to see Esther. He was five days old and ten pounds! Esther said, "Oh, my gosh! He's half grown already!" Now he is six foot three inches. Philip also has a lot of these same sensitivities Rachel has. The name Philip means "lover of horses, gentle," and he is a very gentle young man. I have an eighty-seven-year-old friend, and Philip will come and hold her arm to help her walk. He developed this caring attitude from being with me when I was helping Esther.

Esther loved my cooking! I like to cook a lot of Italian specialties, and I love to cook for people. I also did Esther's laundry when I was at her house. She says I was her favorite "bather," because I would take the washcloth and gently go between each toe. Everybody loves a foot rub!

My children loved Esther's cat, Tiggy. She used to sit on the television set and watch them play. My older son, Brian, is almost twenty years old now. One day when he was little, Tiggy slapped him, but he didn't mind; he just thought it was funny! He said, "Oh, the cat hit me with his hand!" Esther and I have laughed over that comment for years.

I am very grateful for the time I was able to help Esther, and I consider that it was a great privilege to be able to do this. My family and I keep the Smiths in our hearts and prayers.

Anne Shriver is a Lilburn artist who loves to cook.

A Mom's Service
Impacts a Daughter

Rachel Shriver

My mother and I share many similar traits. One that we both consider to be very important is a servant's heart. This may have been something I was born with. However, I believe that seeing it come alive through my mother had an lasting effect on what I want to do with my life. I will never forget going to Esther's house with my mother and my two brothers when I was quite young. We would sit on her big couch and watch old movies on her TV while my mom worked endlessly with Esther, doing anything she could to make her life a little more comfortable. Her tireless effort never went unnoticed or unappreciated by Esther. Even though she could not express it, her gratitude was insurmountable. She did not have to say anything at all; we just knew it was there. Never in my life did I see my mom more energized or joyful than in those three years we spent with Esther. The daily happiness she received from cooking, cleaning, and bathing Esther was apparent to her friends and especially to her family. She often explained to us how much she received back from giving to this precious woman. I never fully grasped this concept until my teenage years, when I began my own service projects. I then gave back to others just as my mom did so many years before. Our family will never forget Esther, not because of how much we did for her, but because of how much she did for us, and the incredible impact she made on us.

Rachel Shriver is the daughter of Esther's friend Anne and a senior in high school. She attends Calvary Chapel in Stone Mountain and plans on attending Auburn University next year.

Esther Outcared Us All

Sue Burton

There are many things I could say about Esther. She is a constant inspiration to me. My main memories stem from the year or so that I helped care for her once a month with several other ladies in the church. What a blessing that time was! Many of us have cared for Esther over the years, but I think she "outcared" us all. I never came away from her house without thinking, *I received more from her than I gave.*

We talked for hours. She was always ready to gently advise me about my four children. That was about twelve or thirteen years ago, and we had two teenagers at home. Ryan and Whitney were both handfuls, and Esther always steered me in a godly direction. Best of all, we prayed together, and I knew that even after I left, she continued to pray for my family and me.

Another memory is the Christmas lunch Esther would orchestrate every year. I would see people there whom I didn't know had helped Esther and I would be amazed. One year my mom came with me. It was a great opportunity to expose her to Christ in action since she was not a believer.

I love seeing Esther at church. Those she loves and who love her always surround her. Joel is her constant, smiling companion. What an inspiration he is to me also! His faithfulness and love for her are examples to all of us. I cannot imagine Lilburn Alliance Church without Joel and Esther Smith.

Sue Burton, a sixth grade teacher at Providence Christian Academy where Joel works, is also a member at Lilburn Alliance Church where Joel and Esther attend.

My Faithful Friend

Ann Cooper

I had the privilege of helping Esther for a short time after we began attending Lilburn Alliance Church about seven years ago. It always amazed me that Esther was never filled with self-pity. It would have been so easy to be. She made me comfortable with her disabilities and taught me how to care for her. She is always concerned for others and their needs and is such a prayer warrior! The love of the Lord shines through her continually.

Thank you, Esther, for the example you have been to me of God's amazing grace that is sufficiently given day by day as we walk with Him. Steve Green's song "Find Us Faithful" is being lived out in your life. "All who come behind you will find you faithful!"

Ann Cooper, a member of Lilburn Alliance Church and a clerk at Lawrenceville Elementary School, is also a wonderful artist.

In Helping Esther,
We are Blessed

Sherry Hartley

Dear Esther,

I'll always remember the first time I went over to your house. Linda Smith had asked me if I would be willing to come over and help you, and I didn't quite know what to expect. I know it had to be harder on you to have this new pastor's wife coming over to assist you than it was on me. You were so gracious and kind. You made me feel so welcome, and you were patient with me as you told me step by step how to help you. I know this took great faith on your part. I remember thinking how you had to go through this process with each of the women who came to your home daily.

After we got you ready for your day, we talked about our families and had a wonderful time sharing, praying, and eating lunch together. Each month when I came back, you would ask about the things we had talked about before, and I knew you had been praying for us. That is what I appreciate the most. To know you pray for Fred and me and our children is a blessing for which I am most grateful. You genuinely care about each of your friends, and you are faithful to pray for them.

I have always been touched by how cheerful and pleasant you are. I know that you daily rely upon God's strength and His enabling to help you through each new day. Whenever I visit you, I am the one who is blessed. I am encouraged to see how you face life's challenges with faith, courage, and a positive attitude.

Thank you for being my friend and for praying for me. Thank you for being God's instrument of encouragement and blessing to me, my family, and our LAC church family. May God bless you indeed and enlarge your territory. May His hand be with you, and may He keep you from evil that you might not cause pain *(Prayer of Jabez,* 1 Chronicles 4:10).

Love in Jesus,
Sherry Hartley

Sherry Hartley, who resides in Lilburn, is the wife of Fred Hartley, pastor of Lilburn Alliance Church. She and her husband have four children, and she is an avid tennis player.

Esther's Projects

Diana Wagner

I started to help take care of Esther later than many of her other friends. It was during the end of the time that Linda Smith was still scheduling women to come in every day and bring something for lunch. I'm not sure of the year, perhaps it was 1994, but I know Esther was still getting up on crutches to walk down the hall to the family room.

I have always been impressed with Esther's determination and positive attitude. I don't know how a person walks without a hip on one side, but Esther did it. As the years progressed and adjustments had to be made, the one thing that could not be rendered inactive was Esther's mind—as she thought up all kinds of projects for us to do.

Looking back over the long list of friends and helpers to Joel and Esther, one could point to a specialty that each one had. One person could cut Esther's hair or organize her papers. Another would do wash or put up wallpaper. Since the arrangement for caregivers changed and she has someone to take care of her personal needs, my role has been more of "project coordinator." We have sorted out closets and cleaned up porches, fought the ever-present battle of the paper monster and dared to dream big sometimes. It seems that God brought the kids at Providence along to fulfill some of those dreams. They have been real encouragers and have accomplished much.

Esther is always interested in what is going on with the kids or my parents and is a good prayer partner. Esther's daughter, Deana, and my daughter, Rachel, have become friends. It is too bad they live so far away from each other now. Esther will always be a mom no matter how old her daughter gets. Her role has changed now from advisor to prayer warrior.

I think what has left the biggest impression on me since working with Joel and Esther is the extreme devotion that Joel has to Esther. He has had twenty-four-hour duty for many years now, and it is beginning to take its toll. I have never heard Joel complain or feel sorry for himself. He has truly laid down his life for another.

I'll close with a funny incident I remember from my early days of helping Esther. When I would come over with lunch, I wanted to make the best use of my time and do some housework or something for Esther. One time I emptied the dishwasher. I found out the next time I visited that I had put away a whole dishwasher load of unwashed dishes! Joel does a good job of rinsing the dishes evidently. Esther was chuckling so much about it that she could hardly get the story out. I don't think I've emptied the dishwasher since!

May God's richest blessing be on Joel and Esther.

Diana, her husband, and four children left Ohio eleven years ago to settle in Georgia. She is a part-time nurse.

The Rookies

Esther Ministers to Teenagers

Barbara Hanak

J oel and Esther have been a gift from the Lord to me and many of the students at Providence Christian Academy. Esther has given us the opportunity to give of our time to see a woman who loves the Lord and trusts in Him through the most difficult of circumstances. Her frequent response is, "God is so good to me."

I met Esther through working with Joel at Providence. She was at the point of needing additional assistance at home when Joel worked late at the school. I went over to visit Esther one afternoon after school and was so surprised to see how grateful she was for the visit and later to see how sharp she was at remembering so many of the details of my life that I had shared with her.

Over a period of several months, students were unable to meet Esther's great need for help. Sports after school, transportation, and schoolwork seemed to interfere continually for those students who had the best intentions. However, several students were able to help with lawn work and house cleaning that first year, and Esther and I developed a friendship.

One of the most significant times for me was when my daughter, Ashley, and I took a small basket of fruit to her for Thanksgiving. We went a day before the holiday, which, unbeknownst to us, was Esther's birthday. When we entered the room where she had been napping, she greeted us with such a big smile. She was so grateful and told us about the time when she had really doubted God's love and care because she was so alone. She had prayed and prayed asking God why He had forgotten her. Suddenly, a big red cardinal, her favorite bird, flew up and sat on her windowsill just looking at her. God showed her that she was important to Him. That same day, a friend called her up and asked if she could come over and bring a hot dog to share for lunch. Esther was convinced of God's love. She told Ashley and me as we stood there, "God is so good to me. I have so much to be thankful for." We were truly humbled and touched and returned home so grateful for what we have!

Joel and I became good friends because my office at school was the maintenance staff closet! Joel would help himself to my candy jar and then very generously fill it up with top-of-the line chocolates—everyone's favorites. He was so thoughtful. One time he gave me a dollar to take my daughter out for Chic-Fil-A lemonade after a long day at work.

The second year I knew the Smiths, Sherri Stewart came to Providence as an eighth grade English teacher. She provided a perfect channel for communication with students as she shared with them her heart to serve. Her eighth grade class decided to "adopt" Joel and Esther as a special family for Christmas. Thus began a relationship between school and the Smiths that has blessed everyone involved over the last two years.

When the eighth graders visited Esther for Thanksgiving, they took her food and wood to heat her house. One of the student's mother, a physiotherapist, demonstrated how the students could help exercise Esther's limbs. In the process, this imaginative mother noticed Esther's need for items to make her more mobile, and she told the students that they could easily make them by hand. For Christmas, several of the boys made utensils to fit her hands so she could feed herself more easily. The girls collected and copied all of Esther's recipes from magazines and three by five cards onto larger paper, and put them into a decorated scrapbook covered with plastic so Esther could turn the pages more easily. Other gadgets were included to give her more independence. When about fifteen students went to deliver the gifts, Esther was overcome with appreciation and gratitude and had tears in her eyes as she thanked them.

As the spring arrived, several students did yard work and visited Esther. One afternoon, as some of the girls were taking Esther for a walk, they noticed how dilapidated the driveway was. Her wheelchair got caught on every crack, and some of the driveway had disintegrated down to the dirt. The girls decided then and there that they wanted to pave the driveway for the Smiths.

Reality and the knowledge that they were talking about a several-thousand-dollar job tempered my faith. However, I thought it would be a great project, even if it took them the next four years. Early in the fall of 2000, the same students, now ninth graders, planned out their approach with prayer. God answered in ways that no one could have anticipated. Not only was the driveway paved that very season, but also the students had more than enough money to buy other things the Smiths needed, as well. The students were able to provide a washing machine, a Christmas basket, a cabinet and counters, and a large shed in the back of their yard for storage.

Esther and Joel were so gracious and invited the class over for a cookout that fall. Everyone had a great time as Joel grilled the hamburgers and the students spent time with Esther. We all basked in the Lord's love and provision for us through the Body of Christ.

Barbara Hanak, mother of two teenagers, runs SPEED, a service program, at Providence Christian Academy.

Beyond What We Asked

Julie Hildebrand

During the fall of 2000, the freshman class of Providence Christian Academy earned money to pave the Smiths' driveway to improve the access for Mrs. Smith, who is in a wheelchair. We worked concession stand sales and car washes. God was so good and blessed our efforts more than we could have ever imagined. The original estimate we received on paving the driveway was $3,100. Through the concession stands and the first car wash, we were encouraged as we were about one fourth of the way to our goal. At the Starfest car wash, God sent a gentleman to us who was in the concrete business. He was so touched by our desire to give to the Smiths that he offered to lay the driveway for the just the cost of supplies!

After encouraging us through this man, God did something even above and beyond what we could ask. A father of one of our classmates, who owned a concrete business, offered to pour the driveway free of charge and also to pour a sidewalk with a ramp to the Smiths' front door. When we offered to pay for the materials, he said he wanted us to use the money toward something else for the Smiths. With the money we had earned, we were able to find other ways to serve Joel and Esther. It was so exciting to see God provide!

Julie Hildebrand, a ninth grade student, attends Providence Christian Academy.

Esther's Ministry to Students

Marvlyn Hildebrand

Last year, when my daughter was in the eighth grade at Providence Christian Academy, she came home telling us about the nicest lady she had ever met. She and a few of her classmates had been over to Esther's to help consolidate a recipe book for her. That day, Esther made an indelible impression on our daughter's heart. Later, when she wanted to visit Esther, I had the privilege of meeting a most remarkable woman of God. I was instantly drawn to her and quickly knew that I had a new friend. Esther's love for the Lord shone through her in a truly genuine way, and I was amazed, encouraged, and challenged—all at the same time. A lovely cross-stitched picture of the names of God hangs above her sofa. As she mentioned each name, it was not as if she had simply memorized them, but it was as if she knew the Lord personally in each of those ways. She was speaking of the Lord, her Master.

This friendship, now a year and a half old, is a constant reminder to me of how wonderful it is to know Christ. I see in Esther the tremendous faith she has in the Lord and her acknowledgement that God is in control of our circumstances and lives. I see her obedience to His Word about being joyful in all things. I see an ongoing spirit of thankfulness and recognition of God's daily blessings in her life.

I have seen her love of life and love of others throughout the year I have known her. On several occasions, students in my daughter's class have had the opportunity to visit Esther. Sometimes they clean windows, file papers, plant flowers, mow the grass, haul firewood, or decorate for the holidays. Each time, Esther makes everyone feel so very welcome in her home. She is always prepared for our visits, putting much time and thought into the ways she can make us feel at home. If there is a first-time visitor, she knows it and makes a point to get to know everyone by name. When it's a workday, she makes sure that there's a snack ready and available to refresh those hard at work. The ice cream bars have been a favorite. Esther makes us all feel very special by the way she puts forth extra effort to have the tables set just right with lovely tablecloths and places for everyone when we are eating together. Esther is very hospitable and is truly a delightful hostess when we are at her home.

I cannot recall a time we visited that Esther did not mention her family. She loves Joel and Deana so much, and it is very evident that she is truly thankful that the Lord has blessed her in such a wonderful way.

I was especially touched one day when we were talking about reading the Bible. Esther loves spending time with the Lord through reading His Word, music, and prayer. I peeked one time when we were praying, and her face was glowing! I recall a time when she expressed her desire to spend even more time worshiping the Lord than what she was already doing. She recognizes and knows that He has been with her, in her own words, "every step of the way," and wants to worship Him for that. Her love of God is so far above her circumstances that I have never heard her speak negatively about them. I see the Lord using Esther in big ways to remind and show those of us who know her that our relationship with Christ is the most important thing in our lives.

Marvlyn Hildebrand, mother of two, lives in Lawrenceville, Georgia, and attends Brookwood Baptist Church.

The Lady with an Iron Will

Jan Barton

We hadn't been attending our church for long when I found that one way to learn about some of the members was to read the prayer and praise insert of the church bulletin. One name came up frequently for a period of time, that of Esther Smith, but I had no face as yet to match that name.

Another habit I nurtured while sitting in the church pew, prior to the service, was people-watching. Again, being new, I was always looking for a friendly or even familiar face. Sunday after Sunday, rain or shine, I saw a couple quietly enter and sit in the back, always in the back and always on the aisle, for the woman, small and frail looking, was wheelchair-bound and in the truest sense, physically bound as well. Her husband tended to her with tender devotion. Many stopped on their way in and after church to greet them. I did not, as I, in all my "need" for friendly people, didn't know what to say. So when in September of 2000, I was asked to consider helping Esther Smith with a home exercise program, I surprised myself by saying yes even though I had no idea who this person was. When I knocked on her door for the first time, her husband answered and introduced me to his wife, and the mystery was solved. Esther's name now matched the face of the woman in the wheelchair and it was a wonderfully friendly face. She may not have been able to move much physically, but she had an energy all her own that inspired me.

Over the next few months, working together to try to limber up stiff joints, I learned much about Esther, her family, and friends. What was more valuable, though, was what I learned from her. Yes, she asked for a great deal, and prayed with a faith and expectation that she knew God would hear, but she also gave back. Year after year, she lost more physical independence. She did not, however, lose her love of people and desire to be social. For many years, Esther opened her home to her friends for a pre-Christmas meal that she would prepare. As she lost mobility over time, her daughter would assist. When it looked nigh on impossible to keep up this tradition after her daughter went out on her own, out of love for Esther, friends took over the preparations. Esther, as only Esther could, organized it all. I had the privilege of being a part of this, not only in the preparation aspect, but in being a guest as well.

I may have given some measure of comfort—or discomfort—by moving her limbs, but she gave me as much, if not more, by making me feel a part of a special group of people who were now more than friendly faces. Through these past months, I have learned that our physical shell is just that, a shell. It is what is housed within that makes a difference, the soul and the spirit. For Esther, that has never been more apparent. She has an iron will but has never crowded out the Holy Spirit who continues to lead her in God's way.

Jan Barton, who attends Lilburn Alliance Church, helped with Esther's home exercise program. She works in a school and has three sons.

A Perfect Role Model

Sherri Stewart

There are not many people who have demonstrated perseverance more than Mary Esther Smith. Books have been written about saints who have endured persecution and imprisonment for their belief in Jesus Christ. Countless Christians have lived for years and years in small cells, deprived of nourishment, the human touch of family and friends, and many have endured untold agony and pain. Yet their hope was in their Savior, and the knowledge that someday, God willing, they would be set free either here on earth or in eternity, and they would know that their suffering was not in vain. They endured for the sake of their Lord. Esther Smith can be counted among this noble group of Christians, yet the call on her life followed a different route than many of the suffering saints we hold in high esteem.

Most missionaries can look back on a time, perhaps in a church service or at a revival, when they felt God leading them into a life on the mission field. I've met many who tell of a speaker who seemed to be speaking right to them, and from that moment on, they knew their lives would take a different direction. I haven't known Esther for very long, but I assume that God's call to Esther came when she first discovered that she had a debilitating disease, but I doubt that she heard the call. In fact, she probably wondered why God would allow a young mother to be afflicted to such a degree, and unlike other called saints, she did not have the privilege of choosing a different path. Jonah could run away from Ninevah, but Esther had no choice but to seek God's plan for her life.

After a believer receives his or her call to a certain ministry, usually many years of training follow. The missionary goes to language school, the pastor to seminary, and others attend Bible school, all in an effort to be well prepared to do the tasks required of them. How do those with infirmities prepare for their lives? It seems to me that for those people who have rheumatoid arthritis, Lou Gerhig's Disease, and other diseases that go from better to worse, they have no choice but to become reactive instead of proactive. If they wake up without too much pain or stiffness, they can plan more activities than if they wake up sore. Then they learn to pace themselves and take it easy. They don't need to be entertained as much as the rest of us who find it hard to sit still. They are satisfied with simple pleasures such as a bird outside their window or a letter from a friend. Esther is one such person who receives a great deal of enjoyment from a card or a song.

I don't mean to denigrate any Christian worker for the sacrifices they have made. They have chosen the high road and have forfeited the pleasures that are available to us worldly ones. But it is still a choice. They can change direction, they can take vacations, they can go on furlough or take a sabbatical, and when they reach a ripe old age, they can retire. Not so with Esther. She never gets a day off; she can take a vacation, but the call on her life never leaves her for a minute. Retirement is out of the question. Even Job saw an end to his suffering, and he was rewarded with new-found health, wealth, and a family. That is why Esther is my heroine. For thirty years, she has been a prisoner in her body. Her mind is sharp; but her body constrains her like a vice and does not allow her mobility or any independence. Yet she does not give up. She rules her roost like a general and delegates like the chairman of the board.

An excellent leader builds a team who buys into the vision he has sold it. Esther also has built a team of friends that form her support team. I think her friends have been her lifeline, especially in the years before she received government help. Even now, though, her friends are what sharpen her mind. They give her a link with the outside world. She absorbs every word they say and forgets very little. She appreciates every small gesture, every visit, to the point that one feels guilty that the smallness of the gesture receives so much gratitude. Even excellent leaders realize some degree of turnover in their team, but not so for Esther. Her team of friends has been with her as long as her illness. The ladies have dedicated years to her care. She cannot pay them, yet they remain with her, because she gives them something in return. She allows them to be participants in her struggles. While none of them will endure physically what she has, they get the opportunity and the privilege of knowing her through it. Job's friends reviled him for the sins they thought he must have committed to be in such a situation. Fortunately, Esther has friends who are an encouragement to her, not just for a time, but for many, many years.

I have only known Esther for a year and a half. I met her through a service project that my eighth grade students had undertaken. Joel, her husband and a custodian at my school, cleaned my room every day after the kids had gone home. Many a day we talked about Esther's condition, and he solicited help, knowing that with his work schedule, he couldn't be there for her as much as he would have liked. He asked if we could visit her weekly since she was alone so much.

My students took on the Esther project with gusto. We collected wood for their fireplace because Esther required a very warm house during the winter months. We brought food for Thanksgiving. One of our parents, a physiotherapist, took a handful of students to Esther's and taught them how to exercise her limbs. For Christmas, we made gadgets for her like bent utensils and a large print book of her favorite recipes. After Christmas, Joel asked if we could visit her even more. This we were not able to do, but many families volunteered to come on a monthly basis. That same class, which I no longer teach, has gone on to pave their driveway and buy a shed for them. Esther loves teenagers and showed her appreciation by throwing a barbecue for the kids. She has the ability to communicate with them, so they, too, in their own way, are part of her team.

How does someone like Esther give back to the people who are part of her team? She does it by being attentive. She can listen; she can counsel; she can pray. In the communication, we find a role model of how one who is in pain can minister to others. It's the widow's mite—the most of what she has, she gives.

For me, Esther is the perfect example of an overcomer. In Genesis, Abraham lived in a tent and could only dream of a time when he would live in a permanent home. Esther's tent is a body that confines her, yet her hope is her future home in Heaven where she will be able to move with no constraints. No one will appreciate that more than Esther.

Sherri Stewart, a teacher at the Christian school where Joel Smith works, became involved in Esther's life through a service project that her eighth grade class was involved in.

The Queen

Personal Testimony
October 24, 1992

Mary Esther Smith

My name is Mary Esther Smith, and I have rheumatoid arthritis complicated by psoriasis. I have had it for nineteen years, since my daughter was two years old. I am from Corpus Christi, Texas. I met Joel in California during the Vietnam War. After he got out of the service, we moved here where his family lives. I had always been a very active, high-energy person, and I thought I could do all things by myself. I thought that marriage was the complete fulfillment of a young girl's dreams. After four years, I was disillusioned with marriage, as Joel was not meeting all my emotional needs. I did not realize that what I was really seeking was a personal relationship with God through Jesus Christ—who is the only one who could meet all my emotional, physical, and spiritual needs.

A year later, I was at home from work sick and was watching Phil Donahue. I remember hearing the wife of Pat Boone say how she had prayed to the Lord to restore her marriage. I prayed the same thing, and that was the beginning of my understanding about how God answers prayers. He gave me such a love for Joel that has grown stronger through the years. I also began to understand that a husband could never meet the needs that only God can meet.

At the same time, God gave me Deana, another answer to prayer, as we had been told that it would be a miracle if we were ever able to have a baby. It was at this time that I went forward in church and prayed that God would use me and mold me into His perfect image. Little did I realize that it was going to take much more work than I thought, but when we ask God to take us at our word, He starts that work in us. I began a real search, studying God's Word and praying, seeking His will for my life. I longed to have a closer relationship with Him.

That is when the arthritis began to manifest itself in me. At that time I didn't wonder why God was letting this happen to me because I thought that I would get well. God didn't heal me the way I thought He would. He even did a better job! He gave me joy and peace in the midst of pain and suffering because He said, *"We know that in all things God works for the good of those who love Him, who have been called according to His purpose"* (Romans 8:28).

People say I have a glow and a smile, and yet they know I have a lot of pain all the time. This is what God did for me because I was not normally that kind of person. God gave me many verses along the way that have encouraged me many times when I was having very hard times. He told me He would never leave me or forsake me, and He hasn't.

The devil also tempted me with thoughts of suicide once. The very first time I could not get out of bed was Sunday in about 1975. Joel had left with Deana; I was feeling so desperate with pain. The devil came and said that if I got up and took all those pills, it would relieve

Joel and Deana, and that things would be better for them. I did not have the energy to get up, so I lay in bed, and I started to talk to God.

All of a sudden, John 14 came into my mind. I am not good at memory verses, but at that time, the whole chapter came before my eyes. I could hear it in my mind quoted verbatim to me. I knew it was from God. Certain verses jumped out at me:

> *Do not let your hearts be troubled. Trust in God; trust also in me* (John 14:1).
>
> *I will ask the Father, and He will give you another Counselor to be with you forever— the Spirit of truth* (John 14:16-17).
>
> *Peace I leave with you; my peace I give you. I do not give to you as the world gives. Do not let your hearts be troubled and do not be afraid* (John 14:27).

The whole thing that I got out of it was that He would always be there for me, in the hard times, the good times, and the in-between times. He would never, ever leave me, and I clung to that promise.

That was when the church was praying for me all the time, but they had not begun to help me physically yet. Saundra Brewer, a member of our church, called me up and asked me if I had been having a hard time. She said she had felt an urgency to pray for me during the Sunday school hour, which was the same time that God had given me that chapter in John. That was the first "official" act of ministry of the church to me, aside from praying for me. Saundra began to take me to water exercise classes at the YWCA. I had other friends helping out, including Edna Bryan, formerly of Lilburn Alliance Church, but there were not enough friends to meet all my needs. As I began to get worse physically, I had worn my four friends down to a frazzle! Frances Holland was added to make five friends, so then I had the five days covered.

Saundra began to talk to people at church, and Edna instigated the "Esther Committee." Oh, how God answered prayer! We went to the Lord and prayed that people would want to help me, and God provided. Every year since 1980, God has provided enough people through the church to be with me every day, so Joel would be able to work and Deana could go to school. Over the years, there have been over sixty people who have come and gone in their ministry to me. God has given me so many blessings because He gave me something so important—He gave me friends.

Through the ministry of the church, God not only has met my needs, but He has also given me the desires of my heart. He provided for me always to have medicine and food when I didn't have it; not only just food but prepared food because I was not able to prepare it myself. People of our church have thrown birthday parties for Deana and bought Christmas gifts for Joel and Deana because I couldn't shop. The youth group has cleaned my yard. The church ladies have cleaned my house, done my wash, baked my favorite foods, driven me to doctors, sat with me in the hospital, bathed me, dressed me, and washed and cut my hair. Children have prayed for me and sent me letters and cards of encouragement. I even found a set of encyclopedias in my van one day after church! Yes, the Lord has met all my needs and all my wants. He has done even greater things than I could ever have expected. He has given me love immeasurable. He has given me a wonderful church and devoted friends.

Esther gave this testimonial during a Sunday night service at Lilburn Alliance Church to thank her church family for their help.